D0513767

FOREIGN EXCHANGE EXPOSURE MANAGEMENT
A PORTFOLIO APPROACH

Foreign Exchange Exposure Management
A Portfolio Approach

LUC A. SOENEN

Eindhoven University of Technology,
The Netherlands

SIJTHOFF & NOORDHOFF   1979
Alphen aan den Rijn   The Netherlands
Germantown, Maryland   USA

ISBN 90 286 0309 3

Library of Congress Catalog Card Number: LC 79-65198

Printed in The Netherlands

To my parents

Acknowledgements

This study has benefitted from the help and support of many people. In particular, I would like to thank Professor William L. White of the Graduate School of Business Administration of Harvard University, for his invaluable contributions in guiding the scope and direction of the research, and in the evaluation of the major findings. I am equally grateful to the following members of the Harvard Finance Faculty, Professors R. Glauber, P. Jones and C. Hekman, for their guidance and support. I would also like to express my gratitude to Professor J. Bishop for letting me use his quadratic programming model and for his help in the practical application of the portfolio model.

A special note of thanks is due to all business executives who were contacted during the research. All of these individuals gave very generously of their time and knowledge to make this study possible.

Finally, while it was the support of these many that made this book possible, I alone bear full responsibility for its content and its shortcomings.

Eindhoven   Luc A. Soenen
January, 1979

Table of Contents

X

Chapter I

Introduction

The assets and liabilities of international companies, by definition, are held, and their income stream achieved, in a variety of currencies. Changes in the exchange rates of these foreign currencies may adversely affect the reported profits and the nominal net worth of the company. If the company owns assets denominated in the Spanish peseta and the peseta is devalued relative to the dollar, the dollar value of the peseta assets is altered and so the firm's profits and its net worth changes.

The firm can reduce the uncertainty in these changes by engaging in hedging transactions to cover exposed positions in foreign currencies. These hedging transactions are likely to raise costs to the company. This study focusses on the trade-off between the reduction in foreign exchange risk and the cost of protecting the income or net worth from such exchange uncertainty which hedging can provide.

Field research showed that (a) a number of international companies are still managing foreign exchange on the basis of incomplete and delayed information; (b) dealing with exposure management on a currency by currency basis, i.e., failing to recognize the statistical relationship between the currencies in its foreign exchange portfolio; (c) restricting hedging to the covering of positions which seem to contain down-side risk and leaving uncovered foreign exchange positions which seem to contain up-side potential; and (d) defining the costs of hedging as the spread between spot and forward rates.

All companies interviewed approached foreign exchange exposure management by determining and consolidating the net exposure of the international group per currency, and by estimating future movements of the currencies in which the company is exposed.

However, hedging should be viewed in a different framework, because this measure of risk fails to examine the inherent relationships among the currencies maintained by the company. The international company should consolidate the foreign exchange exposure of all subsidiaries and net out assets and liabilities per currency. Its net exposure will consist of long/short positions in various currencies. This set of foreign currency positions constitutes the currency portfolio of the company. The expected value-variance relationship of the foreign currency portfolio is the framework within which the author views the hedging problem. The multinational company can reduce risk by engaging in hedging. Hedging reduces the exposure and consequently the variance of the foreign exchange portfolio, but also reduces its expected value by the hedging costs incurred.

In this study, the hedging of a currency portfolio is specified as a decision problem, with the company's exposure as input together with spot and forward exchange rates, the future spot rates of the currencies in the portfolio as unknown random variables, and the amounts to be hedged per currency as decision variables. A quadratic programming portfolio model has been written that traces out an "efficient frontier" between the variance of the company's currency portfolio and the expected value of this portfolio at the end of the planning period. For every point of the frontier the program also selects the optimal mix of hedging activities, i.e., the currency position to be hedged and the method of hedging to be used.

Application of the portfolio hedging model to a US multinational firm resulted in the following major findings:

—measuring the costs of hedging as the spread between the current spot and forward rates, results in a substantial overestimate of the costs and subsequently an underhedging of the company's foreign exchange risk.

—When hedging costs are measured correctly, i.e., the sum of transaction costs and the difference between the forward rate and one's forecast of the future spot rate, one can substantially reduce the variance of the company's foreign exchange portfolio at very low cost.

2

—Further substantial reductions in these already small hedging costs can be achieved using cross-hedging, i.e., engaging in a hedging transaction for a particular currency to hedge the exposure in another currency whose price movements are highly correlated to those of the currency of the hedging transaction.

—The principal conclusion is that hedging should be used much more extensively than is the common practice.

The book develops the concept of the portfolio model more fully in chapter II. In chapter III an integrated input to the model, the measurement of exposure, is explored. Chapter IV deals with the random elements in the hedging decision, the assessment of movements in rates of exchange. Chapter V discusses different methods of hedging and related costs. Chapter VI examines the taxation of foreign exchange gains and losses and its impact on the expected value-variance relationship of the foreign currency portfolio. A quadratic programming model using portfolio theory has been developed in chapter VII. The results of a field research on exposure management in fifteen international companies are summarized in chapter VIII. Chapter IX discusses the application of the portfolio hedging model in a corporate environment. Chapter X summarizes the conclusions of this study.

Chapter II

Formulation of the Portfolio Approach to the Hedging Problem

After the international company has consolidated the foreign exchange exposure of all subsidiaries and netted out assets and liabilities per currency, its net exposure will consist of long/short positions in various currencies. This set of foreign currency positions constitutes the currency portfolio of the company.

Traditional foreign exchange exposure management executed on a currency by currency basis fails to recognize the statistical relationship among the changes in the exchange rates of various currencies. However, if the exchange rate movements of two currencies in the portfolio are highly positively correlated, a short position in one currency will largely offset a long position in the other currency. If the currencies were negatively correlated, long positions in both currencies (or short positions) will tend to balance each other out. This kind of exposure netting can be fully exploited in a portfolio model since the overall risk of the currency portfolio is defined as the weighted sum of the variances of the individual positions plus the weighted sum of the covariances among all currencies in the portfolio.

The company has to take a foreign exchange loss (or profit), whether it engages in hedging activities or not. The expected foreign exchange loss (or profit) corresponds to the difference between the foreign currency portfolio valued at the current spot rates and at the expected spot rates at the end of the planning horizon. This argument is not followed by most businessmen, since they mistakenly define costs of hedging as the difference between spot and forward exchange rates. The validity of the Purchasing Power Parity theorem in the form of regular sales price adjustments, may take care of the company's uncertainty with respect to the mean value of

4

its foreign currency portfolio. However, there remains an uncertainty problem to the company, i.e., the variation of the value of the portfolio around its mean.

The objective of foreign exchange management is defined as the minimization of exchange risk to the company, i.e., to minimize the variance of the company's foreign currency portfolio subject to the costs incurred by hedging. Hedging reduces variance caused by exchange rate changes but entails costs to the company. Therefore, we concentrate on the relationship between the expected value and the variance of the company's foreign exchange portfolio at the end of the planning horizon. A portfolio model will be developed to trace out the expected value-variance frontier for the company's foreign currency portfolio. This chapter describes the basics of the portfolio approach to the hedging problem.

A Model of the Portfolio Approach

The hedging problem can be formulated and solved as a decision problem. The data inputs required for the solution of the problem are: (a) a set of known variables, i.e., spot and forward exchange rates, domestic and foreign interest rates; and a set of variables assumed to be known, i.e., the foreign exchange exposure of the company; and (b) a set of unknown random variables, i.e., the future spot exchange rates for every currency in the portfolio at the end of the planning period. The decision variables are the amounts to be hedged in every currency in order to reduce the portfolio's variance to a selected level. These three sets of variables produce an uncertain value, $\tilde{V}$, i.e., the value of the company's foreign exchange portfolio at the end of the planning horizon, with expected value $\bar{V}$ and variance $\check{V}$. The hedging problem is then set up as the minimization of the variance of the portfolio subject to a set of operational constraints reflecting a specified maximum level of hedging costs and bounds on the amounts of hedging transactions. Since the risk factor is expressed in quadratic terms, the solution technique has a quadratic objective function and hence requires quadratic programming. The model then chooses the amounts to be hedged in every currency to produce a desirable combination of expected value and variance. The following flowchart illustrates the inputs and output of the model.

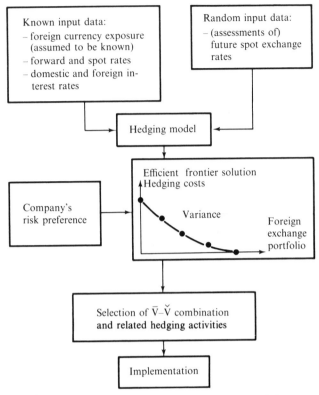

Figure 1. *Inputs and Outputs of the Portfolio Model*

We introduce the following simple notation to illustrate the basic formulation of the hedging problem:

X_i = exposure in currency i, $i = 1, 2, \ldots, N$.

$s_{0, i}$ = spot exchange rate for currency i.

$_0 s_{1, i}$ = forward exchange rate for currency i.

$\tilde{s}_{1, i}$ = future spot exchange rate for currency i.

Δ = transaction costs (assumed to be equal for all currencies).

h_i = amount of exposure in currency i hedged.

$\tilde{V}$ = value of the foreign exchange portfolio at the end of the planning period.

For reasons of simplicity, we limit hedging to the forward market. The value of the foreign currency portfolio at the end of the planning period as a function of the amounts hedged can then be represented as:

$$\tilde{V}(h) = \sum_{i=1}^{N} X_i \tilde{s}_{1,i} + \sum_{i=1}^{N} h_i({}_0 s_{1,i} - \tilde{s}_{1,i} - \Delta \times s_{0,i})$$

or,

$$\tilde{V}(h) = \sum_{i=1}^{N} h_i\, {}_0 s_{1,i} + \sum_{i=1}^{N} (X_i - h_i)\tilde{s}_{1,i} - \sum_{i=1}^{N} \Delta \times h_i \times s_{0,i}$$

The expected value of the foreign exchange portfolio at the end of the period is then:

$$\bar{V}(h) = \sum_{i=1}^{N} h_i\, {}_0 s_{1,i} + \sum_{i=1}^{N} (X_i - h_i)\bar{s}_{1,i} - \Delta \times \sum_{i=1}^{N} h_i \times s_{0,i}$$

or,

$$\bar{V}(h) = \sum_{i=1}^{N} h_i({}_0 s_{1,i} - \Delta \times s_{0,i}) + \sum_{i=1}^{N} (X_i - h_i)\bar{s}_{1,i}$$

The variance of the currency portfolio is:

$$\check{V}(h) = \sum_{i=1}^{N} \sum_{j=1}^{N} (X_i - h_i)(X_j - h_j)\mathrm{Cov}(\tilde{s}_{1,i}, \tilde{s}_{1,j})$$

The maximum expected value and variance of the currency portfolio corresponds to zero hedging. For increased amounts of hedging and hence for larger reductions in expected value due to the incurred hedging costs, the variance of the portfolio decreases and will finally become zero when all initially exposed currency positions are fully hedged. The expected maximum hedging costs are:

$$\sum_{i=1}^{N} h_i(\bar{s}_{1,i} - {}_0 s_{1,i} + \Delta \times s_{0,i}), \text{ with } h_i = X_i \text{ for all } i.$$

Or, the expected value of the fully hedged (i.e. zero variance) foreign currency portfolio is then:

$$\sum_{i=1}^{N} X_i \bar{s}_{1,i} - h_i(\bar{s}_{1,i} - {}_0 s_{1,i} + \Delta \times s_{0,i}), \text{ with } h_i = X_i \; \forall \; i.$$

7

For different amounts of hedging costs, the model allows us to find the related values of $\bar{V}$ and $\check{V}$. The money manager can choose a combination of $\bar{V}$ and $\check{V}$ in dealing with the hedging decision, i.e., in making the trade-off between hedging costs and reduction in portfolio variance. The diagram below illustrates the expected value-variance relationship for different amounts of hedging costs.

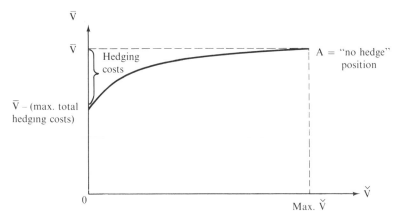

Figure 2. *Expected Value-variance Relationship*

Special Cases of the Portfolio Model

Under the assumption that Purchasing Power Parity[1] and Fisher[2] theorems hold and when there are no transaction costs, the costs of hedging are zero, i.e., $\left(_0 s_{1,i} - \tilde{s}_{1,i} - \Delta s_{0,i}\right) = 0$ for all i since

---

1. The Purchasing Power Parity (PPP) theorem addresses itself to the relation between the domestic price level and the equilibrium foreign exchange rate. The theorem states that changes in relative prices equals the experienced changes in exchange rates. For an excellent discussion of PPP, we refer the reader to Balassa [8], Holmes [41], and Officer [60]. For recent tests of the theory see Aliber and Stickney [4], and Gaillot [31].

2. The Fisher effect in an open economy states that the difference among interest rates of similar assets denominated in different currencies equals the anticipated rate of change in the exchange rate. For an excellent survey article see Officer and Willett in [61].

$\bar{s}_{1,i} = {}_0 s_{1,i}$ for all i and $\Delta = 0$. This means that one can attain the zero variance level at no costs. The corresponding expected value-variance relationship can thus be represented by a flat line. See Figure 3 below.

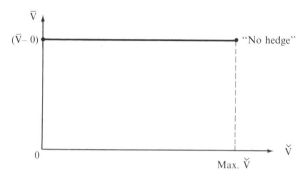

Figure 3. *Expected Value-variance Relationship under Efficient Market Conditions and Zero Transaction Costs*

Under those conditions the "no hedge" strategy leads to:

$$\bar{V}(h_i) = \sum_{i=1}^{N} X_i \bar{s}_{1,i} = \sum_{i=1}^{N} X_i {}_0 s_{1,i}$$

$$\check{V}(h_i) = \sum_{i=1}^{N} \sum_{j=1}^{N} X_i \times X_j \times \mathrm{Cov}(\tilde{s}_{1,i}, \tilde{s}_{1,j})$$

The "hedge" strategy implies:

$$\bar{V}(h_i) = \sum_{i=1}^{N} X_i {}_0 s_{1,i}$$

$$\check{V}(h_i) = \sum_{i=1}^{N} \sum_{j=1}^{N} (X_i - h_i)(X_j - h_j) \mathrm{Cov}(\tilde{s}_{1,i}, \tilde{s}_{1,j})$$

From the comparison of both strategies, it can be seen that the right policy is to fully hedge all exposure, since this leads to a reduction in the variance of the portfolio's variance at no cost.

Under the assumption of efficient markets but non-zero transaction costs, the expected value-variance frontier is no longer a flat line since transaction costs are incurred by hedging exposed positions. An example of such a $(\bar{V} - \check{V})$ frontier is depicted in Figure 4.

9

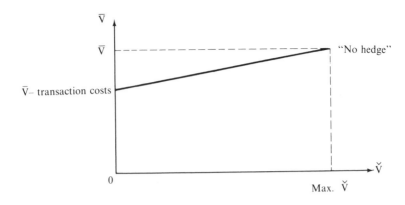

Figure 4. *Expected Value-variance Relationship Under Efficient Market Conditions and Non-zero Transaction Costs*

The "hedge" strategy implies:

$$\bar{V}(h_i) = \sum_{i=1}^{N} (X_i \bar{s}_{1,i} - h_i \times \Delta \times s_{0,i})$$

$$\check{V}(h_i) = \sum_{i=1}^{N} \sum_{j=1}^{N} (X_i - h_i)(X_j - h_j)\text{Cov}(\tilde{s}_{1,i}, \tilde{s}_{1,j})$$

Hedging reduces the variance of the company's foreign exchange portfolio at the expense of incurred transaction costs.

With imperfect markets the hedging costs consist of transaction costs plus the difference between the forward rate and the estimated future spot rate. The $(\bar{V} - \check{V})$ relationship is similar to the one in Figure 2. The "hedge" strategy implies now:

$$\bar{V}(h_i) = \sum_{i=1}^{N} X_i \bar{s}_{1,i} - h_i(\bar{s}_{1,i} - {}_0s_{1,i} + \Delta s_{0,i})$$

$$\check{V}(h_i) = \sum_{i=1}^{N} \sum_{j=1}^{N} (X_i - h_i)(X_j - h_j)\text{Cov}(\tilde{s}_{1,i}, \tilde{s}_{1,j})$$

Every point on the $(\bar{V} - \check{V})$-frontier represents a set of selected hedging activities producing the corresponding combination of expected value and variance.

10

Other Portfolio Models of Foreign Exchange Management

The idea of risk reduction via portfolio diversification has previously been applied to foreign exchange management first by Lietaer [47] and later by Gull [37]. Both models, as our model presented above, consider the variance of the foreign portfolio as an explicit measure of the foreign exchange risk to the company.

The Lietaer model incorporates both foreign exchange and international cash management. Starting from a complete specification of the probability distributions for all currencies in the portfolio and the correlations between them, the model derives an efficient frontier consisting of different financing and hedging strategies. The optimal solution for a specific treasurer is found at the point of tangency between his risk preference curve and the derived efficient frontier.

The Gull paper [37] is limited to the idea of building a currency portfolio applying standard portfolio theory. Gull illustrates how, using a portfolio approach, an efficient risk/cost frontier can be derived and what the implications are of new investments on the composition and value of the company's foreign exchange portfolio.

The Gull model bases the decision-making on historical data, i.e., historical correlation coefficients, and historical mean and standard deviation per currency. The input to our model consists of the actual exposure of the company and assessments of the unknown future spot rates and covariances among them on the basis of the Fisher theorem.

A major shortcoming in application of the Lietaer model is its total dependence on forecasts for all input data (i.e., complete currency scenarios, forward interest rates, cash forecasts; all forecasts are on a monthly basis and six months ahead), which results in an excessive number and sometimes contradictory hedging transactions. The Lietaer model does not explicitly include hedging costs nor does it consider the logistic problems of executing all proposed hedging transactions.

In contrast to both previous models we do explicitly measure and use costs of hedging per individual currency and for three alternative methods of hedging (i.e., the forward market, Eurocurrency market, and the local money market). As the Lietaer model, our hedging model has been applied to a US multinational company.

11

Chapter III

Definition and Measurement of Foreign Exchange Exposure

Foreign exchange exposure management begins with the definition and identification of the international firm's exchange exposure. The end-of-period dollar value of an exposure in any foreign currency equals the multiplication of two uncertain (random) variables, i.e., the amount of the foreign currency exposure and its exchange rate. If $\tilde{X}$ denotes the uncertain amount of the foreign currency exposure and $\tilde{s}$ the uncertain exchange rate, both valued at end-of-period, then the end-of-period dollar value of the foreign currency exposure, $\tilde{V}$, is equal to $\tilde{X}(\tilde{s}) \times \tilde{s}$ or $\tilde{V} = \tilde{X}(\tilde{s}) \times \tilde{s}$. Notice that the amount of foreign currency exposure is itself an implicit function of the exchange rate, i.e., $\tilde{X} = \tilde{X}(\tilde{s})$, since changes in the rate of exchange might affect future cash flows in the foreign currency. In this study, the amount of exposure in every foreign currency is treated as a known variable and the author concentrates on the protection of the dollar value of the foreign currency assets and liabilities against the adverse impact of changes in the rates of exchange. This chapter deals then with the measurement of what we are treating as the "known" variables in the hedging decision problem.

Categories of Foreign Exchange Exposure

There are basically two categories of foreign exchange risk: accounting exposure and economic exposure. The accounting or balance sheet exposure concentrates on how changes in the exchange rates affect the book value of the company. The accounting definition of foreign exposure fails to recognize the market value for many balance sheet accounts and consequently, it does not measure the true value of the firm. The second category of exchange risk, economic exposure, however, deals with the impact exchange rate changes have on the real economic value of the firm. Economic exposure takes into account all actual effects of parity changes. It explicitly considers the future effects of exchange rate movements on investment or profit streams, rather than short-term bookkeeping effects.

We are primarily concerned with the protection of the economic value of the firm. However, in the application of the model in chapter IX, we use both categories of exposure. The following sections examine accounting and economic exposure in more detail.

Accounting Exposure

Balance sheet exposure stems from the maintenance of assets and liabilities in foreign currencies. These items denominated in foreign currencies must be translated into the domestic currency for financial statement preparation and stockholder reporting.

Until recently, accounting for foreign exchange exposure has been characterized by the freedom allowed by the accounting profession about the conventions determining which individual financial items of subsidiaries are translated at historic or spot rates. Although five methods of translating foreign currency into US dollars were approved by juridicial and administrative ruling in the USA (see Ravenscroft in [69]), actually only two methods were used in practice. These principal conventions were the working capital (also called current/non-current) method and the monetary/non-monetary method. The current/non-current method was especially popular prior to 1976. The essential difference between the methods lies in the treatment of inventory and long-term debt. Under the current/non-current method, inventory is exposed to the immediate impact of exchange rate changes and consequently translated at the spot rate, but long-term debt is not. Under the monetary/non-monetary method, inventory may not be exposed, but long-term debt is.[1]

---

1. For a more detailed analysis and illustrative examples, see Lieberman [49], Peterson [62], Prindl [67, Chapter 2].

The Financial Accounting Standards Board (FASB) put an end to the diversity of generally accepted translation methods, by issuance of a standardized reporting system for translating assets and liabilities denominated in foreign currencies, i.e., FASB No. 8 [22]. FASB No. 8, operative since 1 January 1976, dictates which balance sheet accounts are exposed and when losses and gains are to be realized. The new accounting convention differs only slightly from the monetary/non-monetary translation method. Basically, all accounts which are carried at past prices are to be translated at historical rates, and all accounts carried at current prices or future prices (e.g., forward contracts) are translated at current rates. The major impact of FASB No. 8 focusses on the inventory and long-term debt accounts. In determining the translation of inventory, the historic cost of inventory at historic exchange rates will be compared to market value translated at current exchange rates and the lower will be adopted in accordance with the traditional accounting rule of " cost and market whichever is the lower." Long-term debt is translated at current rates. This latter rule has far-reaching impact on companies heavily financed by long-term local borrowing. Translation of the total amount of long-term debt outstanding at current rates could lead to large reported exchange losses (gains) in case a revaluation (devaluation) of the foreign currency occurred.

The current FASB conventions for translating foreign assets and liabilities into dollars assume that the purchasing power parity theory holds, and that the Interest Rate Parity theorem does not hold. Non-monetary items are considered exposed (with the exception of the portion of inventories carried at current prices) to exchange losses, while monetary items are exposed to such losses. The use of the historical exchange rate to measure exchange exposure of non-monetary assets rests on the belief that exchange losses and changes in the local currency prices of these assets are largely offsetting. Thus property and plant and equipment accounts are considered as not exposed, on the generally accepted assumption that their value will usually rise in proportion to the devaluation of the local currency.

Using the current exchange rate to measure the exchange exposure of a firm's monetary assets and liabilities, long-term debt for example, implies the rejection of the proposition that changes in exchange rates are reflected in the relative interest differential in interest rates on similar assets denominated in several currencies (Fisher theorem). However, the author believes that the reported exchange losses resulting from translating, for example, outstanding long-term debt at current spot rate represents a pure accounting loss not necessarily corresponding to an economic loss. This translation loss may be recouperated if the company can adjust the prices of the goods sold in the same currency, so that the dollar value of the income stream in local currency is adjusted for the change in the rates of exchange.

In addition to the accounting standards for foreign exchange transactions, FASB No. 8 also specifies that no reserves are permitted as buffers against foreign exchange gains or losses; exchange gains and losses must be included in determining the net income for the period in which the rate changes. A detailed list of major balance sheet accounts and their translation rates is given in Appendix I.

In contrast with the existing official FASB No. 8-translation conventions in the United States, no such accounting convention is available in Europe. Moreover, in many countries outside the US, international companies do not have to consolidate their subsidiaries' balance sheets nor do they have to report a consolidated corporate balance sheet. However, it is current practice to prepare consolidated financial statements, but then for internal use only.

Because of this lack of uniformity of accounting procedures, there exist a multitude of translation methods or practices in European countries. However, the current rate method, also called the "closing rate method", is most often used. This method consists of translating all foreign currency exposures at the current exchange rate (spot rate) as of the closing date for the company's balance sheet. It is also usual practice to establish separate reserves as buffers against eventual foreign exchange losses. This latter practice is now prohibited in the USA as part of the FASB-conventions.

The lack of uniform translation rules, together with the possible exemption from complete reporting of a consolidated corporate balance sheet and the allowance of reserves against adverse impacts of exchange rate changes upon the company's balance sheet items, leads to the potential danger of a, at least partial, neglect of the foreign exchange exposure problem by European international companies.

Economic Exposure

In practically all cases, translation of balance sheet items does not provide us with a true statement of the actual foreign exchange exposure in any company. Accounting exposure is related only to the effect of parity changes upon the current period value of the assets and liabilities. Accounting exposure management is thus by definition static and historically oriented, since it does not consider the future effects of exchange rate changes. These effects have to be considered in the short-term on a company's liquidity and in the long range in its impact on the entire business operations. The whole range of such risks impinging upon the true economic value of the firm is called "economic exposure".

Identification of economic exposure requires analysis beyond the balance sheet, i.e., future operations or cash flows need to be brought into the analysis. For example, economic exposure can arise as the impact on future sales of a company situated in a country whose currency has appreciated or as the adverse impact on future profits where the local currency has depreciated.

To illustrate the fact that economic exposure goes beyond the balance sheet, consider the following current situation.[2] A US multinational company lends its French subsidiary dollars. This loan will not be included in the company's accounting exposure as (1) such intercompany accounts are excluded upon consolidation; and (2) the loan is denominated in the currency in which the balance sheet is consolidated. However, to the French subsidiary, this represents an economic exposure which could have serious operating effects if the French franc depreciates against the dollar. In extreme cases, the cash losses could impair its liquidity and limit its borrowing capacity during a time of severe credit restriction.

---

2. For other illustrations of the importance of economic exposure, see Prindl [67, Chapter 3].

16

Although we are primarily concerned with the protection of the economic value of the firm rather than its book value, we were not able to satisfactorily quantify all aspects of economic exposure. Therefore, we will use in- and outgoing cash flow forecasts as a proxy for economic exposure and further refer to it as transaction exposure.

Transaction exposure arises from future operations of the company that are contained in the sales and profit plans rather than in the balance sheet accounts. For example, future production and sales in a foreign currency create accounts receivable and accounts payable positions which are exposed to the fluctuations of the exchange rates of the currencies they are denominated. Foreign exchange transaction exposure is thus caused by currency fluctuations between the time transactions are initiated and payments are made. For most companies, the transaction exposure is much more important than the balance sheet exposure, particularly when the company is considered as an on-going business. There are two problems related to the identification of transaction exposure: (1) defining the time horizon over which future cash flows must be assessed. This period will depend on the company's pricing flexibility, its competitive position, or special circumstances (see results of field research summarized in chapter VIII); (2) a fundamental issue suggested by Dufey [16], namely that the forecasted cash flows (receipts and disbursements) must be adjusted for the effects of the expected currency re-valuation. For example, if the foreign subsidiary is producing for exports, then a devaluation of the local currency should improve its sales revenues. However, the subsidiary's revenues may not receive the full benefit of the devaluation because of increased competition from other exporters.

Remarks

Under the hypothesis that both Purchasing Power Parity and Fisher theorems hold, no balance sheet items are considered as exposed to exchange losses, and consequently accounting exposure

17

is zero. Non-monetary balance sheet accounts would be considered non-exposed because their commodity price will be adjusted in proportion to the change in the value of the local currency. The monetary accounts of the balance sheet would be unexposed to changes in the exchange rates due to the validity of the Fisher theorem.

However, although national interest rates, changes in relative price levels, and exchange rates are related, the Purchasing Power Parity and Fisher theorems may not hold precisely. Central government intervention to maintain exchange parities under a pegged rate system, despite increases in relative prices, may lead to lags in the relationship between changes in prices and changes in the exchange rate. Exchange rates may also change for structural reasons, e.g., a sharp increase in exports as a result of mineral discoveries or technological innovations. Hence, accounting exposure cannot be totally ignored and will also be considered as part of total exposure in the application of the portfolio model in chapter IX.

Moreover, most of the time, the company cannot take the exchange loss implied by its translation exposure because these are reflected in its public financial statements. This kind of risk can be considered quite serious by management because a large translation exchange loss may be interpreted by the financial community or stock market as the result of poor financial management and may hurt the image of the company or embarrass its management. However, hedging of accounting exposure should be limited to a minimum only to avoid possible unfavorable impact on earnings per share. This need for hedging balance sheet exposure will disappear as the market gets smarter and more efficient so that it discounts translation exchange losses as an essential cost of doing business abroad. Ideally, corporations should manage their net exposure in terms of the effects of exchange rate movements on future cash flows (transaction exposure).

Chapter IV

Assessment of Exchange Rate Movements

The portfolio approach to exposure management requires the specification of the expected future spot rate at the end of the planning period in order to measure the expected costs of hedging (see next chapter) and the expected value of the portfolio. In addition to future spot rates we also need an assessment of the covariances among all currencies in the portfolio in order to measure the risk (variance) of the foreign currency portfolio.

In an attempt to assess covariances among foreign currencies, the author did a concise statistical study trying to derive conditional joint probability distributions of changes in exchange rates with respect to real economic variables. The results of this empirical work are summarized in Appendix II. Because this approach did not provide a practical means for forecasting covariances between exchange rates, future exchange rate movements will be assessed starting from an application of the Fisher theorem under efficient market conditions.

This chapter examines in subsequent sections the efficient market theory and implications for forecasting exchange rate movements, the traditional view of the forward rate as a predictor of the future spot rate, and exchange rate forecasting using the Fisher theorem which will be used later in the model.

The Efficient Market Theorem and Implications for Exchange Rate Forecasting

Recent research by Giddy and Dufey [33], Giddy [32], Fieleke [20], and Frenkel and Levich [27] has presented evidence supporting the

19

hypothesis of efficiency of the foreign exchange market. Only the weak form of the efficient market hypothesis has been tested,[1] i.e., that current foreign exchange rates fully reflect the information implied by the historical sequence of exchange rates. Hence, successive changes in exchange rates are independent of the sequence of past changes in exchange rates. Giddy and Dufey then argue, in contradiction to Teck [87], that the advent of floating exchange rates has reduced to zero the usefulness of any attempt to forecast exchange rate changes. Their assertion is based on the theory of efficient markets which, when applied to the foreign exchange market under freely fluctuating exchange rates, suggests that the present price properly reflects all available information. As in the case of stock market prices, traders and speculators cannot do consistently better than "the market" in predicting exchange rates. So exchange rates react to new information in an immediate and unbiased fashion, and since new information arrives randomly, exchange rates fluctuate randomly. However, we do not believe that the actual system of managed float corresponds to a pure efficient market hypothesis in which exchange rates fluctuate randomly.[2] At least the first two conditions set forth by Samuelson [73] and Mandelbrot [55] in their formal proofs of random behavior of market prices are not fully satisfied; i.e., (a) prices are free to fluctuate; (b) no single trader is able to corner the market, monopolize information or otherwise manipulate prices; and (c) present prices are strongly influenced by expected future prices. Governmental authorities still occasionally intervene to assure an orderly market behavior. The most important international agreement in this context is the "snake" agreement,[3] that is still followed by Germany, Belgium, The Netherlands, Denmark, and Norway. In some countries, the domestic interest rate for borrowers may be implicitly sub-

---

1. In addition to the weak form there also exists a semi-strong and a strong form of efficient market hypothesis. The semi-strong form asserts that all public information is fully reflected in prices (exchange rates). The strong form maintains that not only public information but all information is fully reflected in the prices.

2. There is an important difference in emphasis between the efficient market theory and the random walk. The random walk theory focusses on whether price changes are random, while the efficient market theory concentrates on the amount of information already reflected in the current prices (see R. Glauber [34]).

20

sidized. Thus authorities may maintain a lower interest rate structure than is warranted by increases in the commodity price level.

However, it is a fact that the market reacts extremely fast to new information available to the public, or in other words, that potential gains in the foreign exchange markets are immediately arbitraged away. This means that exchange markets are highly efficient in eliminating unexploited profit opportunities. In other words, one cannot consistently outsmart the foreign exchange market.

The Forward Rate as a Predictor for the Future Spot Rate

Traditionally the forward rate has been considered as the best available forecast of the future spot exchange rate. In normal circumstances, the forward exchange rate is determined by three principal types of traders: (a) commercial traders seeking assurance about the value of future foreign exchange receipts or payments; (b) interest arbitragers in search of the highest return on short-term funds, who internationally transfer spot funds for short-term investment purposes and cover by a simultaneous forward transaction of the same amount in the opposite direction; and (c) speculators willing to bet on the relation between forward and future spot exchange rates. These three types of operations constitute practically all the supply and demand for forward exchange. In times of abnormal disturbance, however, the national authorities may intervene directly in the forward market through forward purchases of their own currencies in order to prevent the forward discounts from widening too much, sometimes in addition to restrictions on interest arbitrage or speculation.

The forward exchange rate is determined by supply and demand for future currencies. The forward premium or discount is, in fact, a

3. The European "snake" agreement is a formal agreement among its member countries to maintain their cross rates within 2.25 percent of each other and float as a group against other currencies. The Benelux countries agreed on an even tighter 1.5 percent fluctuation limit between their currencies, the so-called Benelux mini-snake or "worm".

reflection of expectations on the future spot rate. Consequently, if expectations are correct then the forward rate will not be biased; if they are incorrect the forward rate will differ from the future spot rate but only in the short run. For example, if an individual expects that the spot rate in the next period (say three months from now) will be lower (higher) than the actual three month forward rate, he will have an incentive to sell (purchase) forward exchange and, if his expectations are realized, he will make a per-unit profit equal to the difference between the forward and the expected spot rate. The result of these actions in the market is to move the price of forward exchange toward the expected future spot rate. Since, in the absence of exchange controls, the forward market is highly competitive and rational, speculative funds will continue to enter the market until the price of forward approaches the expected future price of the foreign exchange when these forward contracts come due. Consequently, as suggested by C. Hekman in [39], the forward exchange contains the best prediction of price changes for the contract period as it contains all the information available to the public at any point in time. More precisely, the best estimate of the future spot rate is the current forward rate for contracts maturing on that future date. For example, the best prediction of the rate in one month, three months or one year is the forward rate for contracts maturing in one month, three months or one year. The consequent conclusion is that the forward market provides a viable alternative to risk-averse traders. The forward exchange rate is expected to be a more accurate predictor the more freely speculators are allowed to enter and exit the market and the more readily available the relevant information is to the public.

The forward exchange rate could be a biased estimator of the future spot rate[4] as a result of the thinness of the foreign exchange markets; i.e., when speculative supply and demand are not infinitely elastic. Statistical tests performed by Kaserman [44] proved that

---

4. Using the definition set forth by Kohlhagen [48] the forward rate is said to be a biased estimator of the subsequent spot rate if the resulting profit or loss from a continuous long (or short) position in a currency is significantly different from zero. It follows then that the forward market is unbiased if in the long run the forward rate is not significantly different from the corresponding future spot price.

22

under freely floating exchange rates the forward rate is a biased predictor of the spot rate with the bias depending upon the direction of movement in the spot rate. The bias, although small, is downward in periods when the spot rate is increasing and upward when the spot rate is decreasing. Notwithstanding the statistical evidence of the bias in the forward rate as a predictor of the future spot rate; Kaserman was unable to reject the hypothesis that the forward rate is a " perfect " predictor of the future spot rate in general, neither at the 0.01 nor 0.05 level of significance. But the R^2 of the tested linear relationship between the future spot rate and the forward rate was extremely small $(R^2 = 0.58)$, indicating that there is considerable variation in the future spot rate that is not accounted for by the forward rate. Kohlhagen [48] also found evidence of bias of the forward rate during selected short-term periods. But, surprisingly, he also found evidence that official intervention in the forward market is not a source of bias in the forward rate. Periods of extensive official interference in the forward exchange market were in fact associated with an unbiased forward rate. In a later article Kohlhagen [49] and also Ethier [19] argued that the forward rate has remained an unbiased predictor of the future spot rate under the floating rate period. However, although the average forward premium (or discount) has not been larger than in the fixed rate period, Kohlhagen found evidence that the standard deviation of the mean difference between the forward and future spot rates is in most cases twice as large as under the fixed exchange rate system. In summary, the author feels that the research evidence indicates that the assumption that the forward rate is an unbiased predictor of the spot rate is a reasonable working assumption. Consequently, forward rates could be used as estimates of the future spot rates. Since forward rates do not exist for all currencies, however, this procedure is not universally applicable. For that reason, an alternate procedure is proposed, the Fisher theorem.

Exchange Rate Forecasting Based on the Fisher Theorem

Recently, Levich [50] tested the ability of four models in forecasting spot exchange rates. The models tested are: (a) Fisher domestic or

Interest Parity theorem using treasury bill rates; (b) Fisher external or Interest Parity theorem using Eurocurrency deposit rates; (c) the forward rate as a predictor of the future spot rate; and (d) random walk model with zero drift or using the current spot rate as a predictor for the future spot rate. The forecasting period consisted of 430 weeks covering the period of 1 March 1967 to 5 September 1976. There was some evidence that forecast errors become smaller as the managed float continues in general. In reference to the section above, the results proved that the predictive power of the forward rate definitely declined over the sample period. However, in many cases, the forward rate was an unbiased forecast of the future spot rate. Their results further indicated that overall the Fisher model (especially the external version) leads to a greater number of unbiased or smallest bias forecasts among the four models tested. This conclusion has further been affirmed by Giddy [32], as he concludes that "in the absence of predictable exchange market intervention by central banks, the interest rate differential is the best possible forecaster of the future spot rate."

For these reasons and also because of the more ready availability of test data, the author opted for the use of the Fisher model to produce forecasts of future spot rates and to be used as a starting point for derivation of a covariance matrix of currency comovements. Moreover, for all heavily traded currencies, both the forward rate and the Fisher model lead to an identical forecast of the future spot rate, since interest rates and forward and spot exchange rates are determined simultaneously in the money and foreign exchange markets.

The Interest Rate Parity theorem states that covered interest arbitrage will eliminate any covered interest rate differentials between equivalent interest-bearing securities denominated in different currencies. Let us introduce the following notation:

$s_{0,i}$ = current spot exchange rate of currency i in terms of domestic currency (assumed to be the US dollar) per unit of foreign currency i.

$E(\tilde{s}_{1,i})$ = expected exchange rate of currency i at the end of period ONE.

r_i = one-period interest rate on assets denominated in foreign currency i (domiciled in country i).

$r_\$$ = one-period interest rate on domestic (US) currency assets.

Then, according to the Fisher theorem or Interest Rate Theory of Exchange Rate Expectations, the following statement must hold:

$$\left\{ \begin{array}{l} \text{Value at end of period} \\ \text{ONE of \$A earning} \\ \text{interest rate } r_\$ \end{array} \right\} = \left\{ \begin{array}{l} \text{Value at end of period} \\ \text{ONE of \$A converted into} \\ \text{foreign currency } i \text{ and} \\ \text{earning interest } r_i \text{ until} \\ \text{it is converted back at} \\ \text{the end of period ONE} \\ \text{into \$ at the expected} \\ \text{future spot rate, } E(s_{1,i}). \end{array} \right\}$$

$$A(1 + r_\$) = \left(\frac{A}{s_{0,i}}\right) \times (1 + r_i) \times E(\tilde{s}_{1,i})$$

$$\frac{1 + r_\$}{1 + r_i} = \frac{E(\tilde{s}_{1,i})}{s_{0,i}}$$

$$\Rightarrow E(\tilde{s}_{1,i}) = s_{0,i} \times \left(\frac{1 + r_\$}{1 + r_i}\right)$$

subtracting 1 from each side of the equation $1 + r_\$/1 + r_i = E(\tilde{s}_{1,i})/s_{0,i}$:

$$\Rightarrow \frac{r_\$ - r_i}{1 - r_i} = \frac{E(\tilde{s}_{1,i}) - s_{0,i}}{s_{0,i}}$$

if r_i is small with respect to 1.0, then to a close approximation,

$$\frac{E(\tilde{s}_{1,i}) - s_{0,i}}{s_{0,i}} = r_\$ - r_i$$

or

$$E\left[\frac{\tilde{s}_{1,i} - s_{0,i}}{s_{0,i}}\right] = r_\$ - r_i$$

The above equation says that the expected rate of change in the exchange rate of currency i is equal to the interest rate differential of identical assets denominated in currencies i and \$. The interest rate differential can therefore be used as a forecaster of future exchange rates because foreign exchange markets, at least for major currencies, are highly efficient and competitive in nature, in which present

25

rates properly reflect all available information. So that the market's expected rate of change of any exchange rate is reflected in interest rate differential between the two currencies.

There might be deviations from the interest parity line due to transaction costs and/or less than infinite elasticities of demand and supply of foreign exchange.[5] Frenkel [25] illustrated that these deviations fall into a "band" around the interest parity line. Within this band, the points which are off the traditional interest parity line may still be interpreted as equilibrium points. The existence of elasticities which are less than infinite will widen the neutral band and will therefore account for a larger percentage of the deviation from the interest parity line. The elasticities computed by Frenkel were extremely low relative to the notion of the highly competitive nature of the market, if no allowance was made for transaction costs. In a later article, Frenkel and Levich [27] suggest that the value of the implied elasticities is much higher once estimates of the transactions costs are incorporated and is therefore consistent with the notion of the high degree of competitiveness in the foreign exchange market.

Assessing the Exchange Rate Covariance Matrix

The interest rate parity equation, i.e., $E(\tilde{s}_{1,i}) = s_{0,i} \times (1 + r_{\$}/1 + r_i)$, has been used to generate the expected value of the future spot rates for seventeen foreign currencies. The final objective of this exercise was to estimate the covariance matrix among the future spot rates. Data on the exchange rate changes for the seventeen foreign countries and the US were taken from several sources, i.e., the International Financial Statistics (IMF), World Financial Markets (Morgan Guaranty Trust Company), Financial Statistics (OECD), and the Federal Reserve Bulletin. A detailed list of the data and sources is given in Appendix III. All spot and money market rates are end-of-month quotations, covering the period June 1971 through December 1976. The means and standard deviations of the ratios of the actual (a_i) over the spot rates as forecasted by the Fisher procedure (f_i) are summarized in Table 1.[6]

---

5. There is a vast literature on the relationship between forward exchange rates and interest rate differentials. Some of the more interesting articles are: Auten [6], Pippenger [63], Prachowny [65], Stein [82], Tsiang [84], and White [86].

Table 1. *Means and Standard Deviations*

Currency	Mean, $m_i = \sum_{i=1}^{66} \left(\dfrac{a_i}{f_i}\right)$	Standard Deviation $= \sqrt{\sum_{i=1}^{66} \dfrac{\left(\dfrac{a_i}{f_i} - m_i\right)^2}{66}}\ (\times 10^{-2})$
AS	0.996	2.974
A$	1.001	3.616
BF	0.995	2.974
C$	1.001	1.345
DG	0.995	3.007
DK	0.994	2.742
DM	0.996	3.105
FF	0.996	2.927
IL	1.003	2.792
NK	0.993	2.581
PE	1.001	2.330
PS	1.003	2.371
SAR	1.004	3.325
SF	0.994	3.428
SK	0.997	2.442
SP	1.000	2.070
Y	0.996	2.172

---

6. Throughout the book, the following notation will be used for foreign currencies:

AS : Austrian Schilling   NK : Norwegian Krone
A$: Australian Dollar   PE : Portuguese Escudo
BF : Belgian Franc   PS : Pound Sterling
C$: Canadian Dollar   SAR : South African Rand
DG : Dutch Guilder   SF : Swiss Franc
DK : Danish Kroner   SK : Swedish Krona
DM : Deutsche Mark   SP : Spanish Peseta
FF : French Franc   Y : Yen
IL : Italian Lira $: US Dollar

Table 2. Covariance Matrix ($\times 10^{-4}$)

	AS	A$	BF	C$	DG	DK	DM	FF	IL	NK	PE	PS	SAR	SF	SK	SP	Y
AS	8.84																
A$	2.40	13.08															
BF	7.39	2.63	8.84														
C$	1.13	2.37	1.34	1.81													
DG	7.42	2.81	8.5	1.16	9.04												
DK	7.05	2.49	7.57	1.37	7.51	7.52											
DM	8.16	2.66	8.67	1.31	8.65	7.88	9.64										
FF	6.44	1.76	6.85	1.28	6.76	6.52	6.93	8.57									
IL	2.91	0.75	3.08	0.50	3.50	3.00	2.98	4.40	7.80								
NK	5.88	1.92	6.18	0.95	5.91	5.82	6.42	5.05	2.04	6.66							
PE	5.35	1.66	5.65	0.76	5.74	5.34	6.0	5.24	2.94	4.17	5.43						
PS	2.53	0.67	3.54	0.18	3.50	3.09	3.34	3.48	2.30	2.55	3.22	5.62					
SAR	3.58	1.90	3.52	-.12	3.64	3.47	3.79	2.78	1.04	3.01	2.69	2.38	11.06				
SF	7.37	2.57	7.82	1.05	7.64	7.15	8.26	6.81	2.98	5.95	5.26	2.64	3.50	11.75			
SK	6.10	1.40	6.69	1.20	6.55	6.20	6.87	5.87	3.31	5.03	4.58	2.83	2.35	5.92	5.96		
SP	2.98	1.53	2.94	0.25	2.94	3.06	2.83	3.05	1.68	2.53	2.09	0.92	1.95	3.21	2.37	4.28	
Y	3.30	2.20	3.91	0.86	3.80	3.92	3.77	4.01	2.57	2.54	2.90	2.28	2.06	3.81	2.84	1.95	4.72

The covariance matrix for the seventeen foreign currencies is derived applying the standard formula:

$$\mathrm{Cov}(i, j) = \frac{1}{n} \sum_{i=1}^{N} \left[\left(\frac{a_i}{f_i} - m_i \right) \times \left(\frac{a_j}{f_j} - m_j \right) \right].$$

This formula has been applied with $m_i = 1.0$, assuming that the forecasting procedure provides unbiased estimates. The resulting covariance matrix is given in Table 2.

Chapter V

Hedging Techniques and Costs of Hedging

When considering hedging decisions, the treasurer must evaluate the availability and relative after-tax costs of alternative methods of hedging to determine which type of hedge is the most appropriate for a given exposure. However, the final decision whether or not to hedge, will be determined by a trade-off analysis between the costs of cover and the implied reduction in foreign exchange risk to the company.

Methods of Hedging

Several hedging techniques are available to the international company. The choice among them is determined by their relative availability, costs and the amount to be hedged.

Leading and lagging has probably become the most favored of all corporate hedging alternatives. In some cases, leading and lagging is done on a continuous basis to reduce the impact of projected important changes in currency values on net exposure, i.e., to protect long positions in devaluation-prone currencies (e.g., accelerating the collection of A/R) or to speculate on an eventual up-valuation (e.g., decelerating A/R retrieval and accelerating A/P payments in the up-valuation-prone currency). In case of accelerated payments of the foreign subsidiary to the parent company, the " leads and lags " action has a direct cost to the leading subsidiary and an opportunity gain to the receiving or lagging parent. The quantifiable costs consist of the interest paid, or foregone, by the foreign subsidiary, depending on whether the subsidiary has to borrow the accelerated funds locally or has the cash already on its books, and the interest yield of the recipient parent company, if those funds can in fact be put to use. Lagging payments due to the subsidiary from the parent or other subsidiaries has the same equivalent cost. This, of course, represents only the quantifiable costs of "leading and lagging". It also involves the large intangible costs of upsetting the subsidiary's customers or its suppliers, and the intangible cost of interfering with the local subsidiary's operations and profitability.

Besides, the range of the technique may be limited because it is controlled to some extent by the foreign exchange control authorities. Intercompany transfers assume one hundred percent ownership of the various corporate subsidiaries so that independent minority stockholders of a single subsidiary are not hurt.

Because it is impossible to define the full costs of the "leads and lags" techniques, we examined only the company's net exposure after leading and lagging has been exploited as far as the individual company deems it desirable. Moreover, the importance of the "leads and lags" procedure is overaccentuated regarding its impact on the total exposure of the international group. Only relatively small positions can be covered in such a way, since it is essentially limited to A/R and A/P management. Therefore, the following discussion is restricted to three principal methods of hedging, i.e., hedging in the forward market, Euro-currency market, and the local money markets.

Although, as will be shown in the next section, hedging costs are very similar across the three hedging techniques, firms usually prefer to hedge their foreign exchange exposure in the forward exchange market rather than in the Euro-currency or local money markets. There are at least five reasons why international companies might favor the forward market as method of hedging:

—Forward transactions are off-balance sheet items, while local borrowing appears on the balance sheet and consequently affects the company's debt/equity ratio.
—The forward market is very flexible; one can easily change the amount and dates of the forward contracts. One can also relatively easily extend the bounds on the volume of forward contracts; while in the case of borrowing everything has to go through the ordinary loan department of the bank and changing

the limit of the line of credit would involve a complete renegotiation of the loan. Hence, transaction costs are smallest for hedging in the forward market. With respect to the Euro-currency market, the forward market also offers much more flexibility, since hedging in the Euro-currency market is practically restricted to a few major world currencies and the minimum amount of any transaction is relative very high (e.g., $ 1,000,000 equivalent).

—Under the forward market contract no cash has to be paid until the actual maturity date of the contract; while under local borrowing interest payments have to be made along the way.

—Large amounts are better dealt with in the forward market. Hedging of large exposures would definitely require a renegotiation of credit lines. Often, local borrowing is used for hedging purposes as a way to keep good banking relations, especially at times when no short-term financing via overdraft facilities is needed.

—Hedging operations are subordinated to the main business activities of the company; i.e., manufacture and sale of its products. Foreign lines of credit might not be used or only for a small fraction for hedging purposes because these overdrafts are the principal source of short-term financing to the company. Companies want to leave lines of credit open and will use up this source for hedging only in exceptional cases of foreign exchange requirements.

Definition of Hedging Costs

The cost of hedging in the forward market or through the money markets ought to be defined as the difference between the value one would receive at the end of the period if one did not hedge and the amount that would be received if one did hedge. The cost of hedging in the forward market is, therefore, the difference between the future spot rate and current forward rate plus any transaction cost associated with the forward contract. Since at the time of the decision, the future spot rate is uncertain, the costs of hedging in this way are, in part, uncertain. The expected costs of hedging in this manner are the expected value of the difference between the (known) future spot rate plus the known transaction cost. If the expected future spot rate is different from the current forward rate, then the expected cost of hedging becomes the transaction cost plus this expected difference. If the current forward rate is an unbiased estimate of the future spot rate, the expected cost of hedging in the forward market is just the transaction cost associated with the forward transaction.

The costs of hedging through the money markets are the difference between the interest rate differential in the two currencies and the spread between the current and future spot rate of the foreign currency plus any transaction costs. Since the future spot rate is uncertain, the costs of this type of hedging are uncertain as well. The expected costs of hedging in the money market are the transaction cost plus the difference between the interest rate differential and the expected value of the difference between the current and future spot rates. If the interest differential is equal to the difference between the current spot rate and the current futures rate, as it most often is, and if the futures rate is an unbiased estimate of the future spot rate, however, the expected cost of hedging through the money markets is only the transaction cost involved.

This definition of the costs of hedging is not the one used by many international companies. These companies often consider the cost of hedging, in, say, the forward market, as the difference between the current spot rate and the current forward rate. Only one company out of a sample of fifteen companies interviewed (see chapter VIII) defined the cost of hedging correctly. However, assuming efficient foreign currency markets and ignoring transaction costs, the cost of a forward hedge is zero, since either way, with or without hedging, you end up with the same expected return.[1] As an example, suppose outstanding Italian Lira receivables are covered by selling the IL forward at a ten percent discount. The company is sure to collect the receivables at the forward rate; this implies a ten percent exchange

---

1. This statement should be understood in ex-ante sense. " Efficient market conditions rule out unexploited profits " does not imply that ex-post foreign exchange transactions can never be profitable. Rather it implies that ex-ante the market participants behave in such a way as to eliminate all expected profit opportunities.

loss. However, if the company chooses not to cover these IL receipts, it will face a loss whose expected value is ten percent anyhow; since the forward rate is an unbiased predictor of the future spot rate.

Similarly, hedging in the money market consists of borrowing the foreign currency (borrowing US dollars), converting these funds into US dollars (the foreign currency), and investing them in the money market for the same period as the original loan agreement. Especially the countries where there is no forward market for the currency, short-term borrowing is the standard method of reducing long exposed positions. The cost of hedging in the money market is essentially equal to the interest rate differential between the borrowing and the investment rates adjusted for the two currencies involved. Again for most currencies the expected value of the cost of hedging in the money market is zero (in an ex-ante sense), as the Interest Rate Parity theorem holds. It was discussed in chapter III that deviations from the parity line form a neutral band around the parity line within which no speculation is profitable. In efficient markets, both types of hedging should produce similar results at the same costs, because interest rates and forward and spot exchange rates are determined simultaneously. Money and foreign exchange markets respond continuously to one another to achieve equilibrium.

Estimates of Transaction Costs

The cost of transactions in foreign exchange markets is composed of three elements:
(a) brokerage or service fees charged by the foreign exchange dealers (i.e., the ask-bid spread), or in case of borrowing, compensating balance requirements represent an indirect service fee.
(b) Information costs, i.e., all expenses incurred of being informed, such as subscription fees for services as Predex, Reuterreports, foreign exchange counseling, etc.
(c) Administrative costs, i.e., the time cost of the executive(s) in charge of exposure management, the cost of executing hedging transactions such as telephone and telex costs, visits with bankers, etc.

There are no direct estimates of the cost of transactions in the foreign exchange or money market. This makes it extremely hard, if not impossible, to make an accurate estimate of transaction costs. Fortunately, some research in this area has lately been done by Frenkel and Levich [27, 28]. They use data on triangular arbitrage as procedure for the estimation of the cost of foreign exchange transactions. Triangular arbitrage is supposed to keep the cross-exchange rates consistent. As an example, consider the exchange rate between the US dollar and the DM, and the exchange rates between the $ and the SF, and between the SF and the DM. In the absence of transaction costs, consistency of equilibrium in the exchange markets requires that for any particular maturity:

$$\left(\frac{\$}{DM}\right) = \left(\frac{\$}{SF}\right) \times \left(\frac{SF}{DM}\right)$$

The equation indicates that the dollar price of one DM should equal the product of the price of one SF in terms of $ and the price of one DM in terms of SF.

The discrepancy between both sides of the equation is used as an estimate of total transaction costs in the market for foreign exchange. Frenkel and Levich made a distinction between four basic transaction costs. Using their notation:

t = cost of transactions in domestic securities
t^* = cost of transactions in foreign securities
t_s = cost of transactions in spot exchange rates
t_f = cost of transactions in (ninety-day) forward exchange
     rates

Their estimates for the current managed float period (i.e., post-1973) are: $t = 0.03\%$, $t^* = 0.10\%$, $t_s = 0.5\%$, $t_f = 0.5\%$.

The above estimates are used in the application of the model (see chapter IX). This means that transaction costs are assumed to be equal for all foreign currencies but differ depending on the method of hedging. However, in reality, transaction costs will slightly differ especially for the less traded currencies as larger brokerage fees will be charged by the foreign exchange dealers. The major reasons for this simplifying assumption are twofold: it was impossible to collect cross exchange rates between less traded currencies, i.e., the SAR, DK, etc., and because the company on which the model has been applied had equally easy access to all foreign currencies of its foreign exchange portfolio.

It fits in this context to discuss an issue that is relevant to the cost of transactions in the forward market, i.e., the timing of forward exchange contracts. Standard maturities for forward exchange contracts are 1, 2, 3, 6 or 12 months. While it is difficult, longer maturities can sometimes be arranged. It is also possible to write contracts for other (non-standard) maturities but since banks generally find it more difficult to enter into an offsetting transaction the rates quoted may be less attractive. Banks also write option contracts which provide for varying amounts of flexibility concerning the delivery date. Such a contract, for example, might be written to provide for delivery to be made during the first fifteen days of the month at one rate or the second fifteen at another. Again, since this increases the risk to the bank, the cost to the customer is higher. Premature termination of a forward contract is quite possible, then the bank will buy back at the then prevailing rate of exchange the currency originally sold forward to the customer. Similarly, if the bank has bought forward and the customer is unable to deliver the currency, then, on or before maturity of the contract, the bank will sell back to the customer at the prevailing exchange rate of the currency originally bought forward from the customer. A forward exchange contract may also be extended if for some valid reason the customer cannot meet his commitment by the expiry of the original forward exchange contract. This extension is normally done by the bank buying back at the current spot price the currency and then re-selling on the basis of that current spot price adjusted by whatever the forward margin may be. A similar, but reverse, procedure is adopted in the case of a forward purchase contract.

All procedures described above for altering the standard maturities of forward contracts will involve additional transaction costs beyond the ones implied by triangular arbitrage.

Other Considerations

Most published articles that discuss the defensive measures against foreign exchange exposure do not go into the costs in much detail. In

36

order to obtain a better understanding of the types of costs which are practically involved in hedging, the author had lengthy discussions with people of the foreign exchange or international banking department of six large US banks. On the basis of these discussions, I conclude that three factors are important to the use and availability of hedging transactions: (1) the customer (credit-worthiness); (2) the amount of the transaction; and (3) the currency of denomination (the relative availability of the currency).

It is important to emphasize that every bank considered the foreign exchange trading as a service for their commercial customers. US banks customarily charge no commission for this service; instead, they attempt to cover their expenses and to make profits by selling foreign currencies at prices that are marked up from the prices that they pay for the currencies. However, since the competition among foreign exchange dealers is very keen the difference between buying and selling spot rates is very small; e.g., 3 basis points ($ 0.0003) per pound sterling.

We now consider the three hedging cost factors separately.

The Credit-Worthiness of the Company

Before a company can enter a forward contract with a particular bank, the latter will make a careful credit analysis of its customer. In fact, the company usually will have a credit line with the bank. The foreign exchange department specifies definite limits on the amount of any forward contract which can be entered into for a particular customer depending on the evaluation of the company's credit-worthiness. However, the result of this investigation is never reflected in an adjustment of the forward rate actually charged by the bank, because the premium (discount) charged is the actual forward market rate for that currency determined by supply and demand in the forward exchange market. The result of the credit analysis is that upper limits will be defined for all forward transactions with the specific company. For example, assume a company has a two million dollar credit line with its bank. On 2 February it enters a forward contract to buy $ 1,000,000 of DM one month from now and another to sell $ 800,000 worth of IL on 2 May. This means it has utilized $ 1,800,000 of its credit line; i.e., the sum of all outstanding contracts determines the use of the line of credit. As mentioned before the only effect of the credit rating of the company is that it determines the upper bound of forward exchange transactions the bank is willing to undertake without requiring a special check of the customer.

Hedging through the money market will usually involve a more thorough credit investigation of the company, because (a) the borrowing of a foreign currency is handled as any ordinary loan and has therefore to be approved by the loan department of the bank for each transaction separately; and (b) the bank does not have the same flexibility to offset the position it takes for its customer in a particular currency with an opposite currency position as is the case in the forward market. The implications of the credit analysis made by the loan department are that limits are set on the maximum amount of any foreign currency loan to the company and also that, as is the case for domestic currency loans, the customer will be charged a different interest rate (i.e., prime rate + supplement) reflecting his credit-worthiness to the bank. The relevant borrowing and lending rates may be slightly different for different companies. A company may not be able to borrow as much as it might want at a given rate of interest, as it tries to borrow more, lenders may ask a higher rate. Bank credit rationing may pose vague limits on the promptly available supplies of foreign exchange. Actual or feared restrictions on the availability of foreign currency might lead companies to obtain quotes from more than one bank. Field research by Fieleke [21] showed that out of a sample of twenty-four firms, twelve customarily shopped around. The largest variation in quotations reported by these firms was six basis point ($ 0.0006). However, while seemingly a large number of companies request quotes from more than one bank, checking with several banks may influence the market to the detriment of the company by creating an illusion of excessive supply or demand in a given currency. Therefore, firms are often advised to approach only one bank to acquire the desired currency over a period of time on a "best-efforts" basis.

The Amount of the Hedging Transaction

There was general agreement among all foreign exchange dealers of the banks interviewed that there exists a lower and upper bound on the amount of a forward contract below and above which the bank will be reluctant to make a deal. Exceptions might occur when the foreign exchange dealer sees opportunities to bundle several small orders to form a tradable package deal or when he can split up a huge forward contract into several smaller orders among other banks. It is hard to set a single figure for those limits; but the limits would certainly be in the range of $ 100,000 equivalent and $ 200 million equivalent. The previous mentioned field research by Fieleke [21] showed that the range of volume of forward transactions differs vastly from company to company; i.e., three firms claimed to have entered the forward market for a transaction of only 10,000 DM; none of these firms was large. By contrast, one large firm reported that its smallest forward transaction amounted to 32 million DM; several others declared minimum transactions of 1 to 4 million DM.

The upper limit on the volume of foreign exchange transactions can be circumvented by making the contract with several banks, preferably to be executed at different points in time.

All banks also agreed that between both limits the rate charged for a forward contract was a constant equal to the quoted premium or discount (i.e., a constant proportional hedging cost). For reasons of simplicity, we assume that no forward contracts will be available outside both limits, which is what actually happens in most situations. There are exceptions to this general assumption in practice. The bank might be willing to charge the same rate regardless of the amount of the transaction, also when the transaction amount falls outside the usual limits. It is of prime importance to remind the reader that the foreign exchange trading is only part of the business the bank does with a particular company (i.e., other services might include short- and long-term financing, leasing, A/R collection, cash balance management, etc.). Foreign exchange trading is a " service " to the customer, so for a very good (Triple A) customer the bank will do anything to satisfy its customer, i.e., charging him the best rate whatever the amount of the transaction. The bank's foreign exchange trader can try to bundle several small orders to obtain a tradable package of a particular foreign currency. He might also split up an extremely large deal into several forward contracts in order to satisfy his AAA customer. Besides, it is part of the job of a

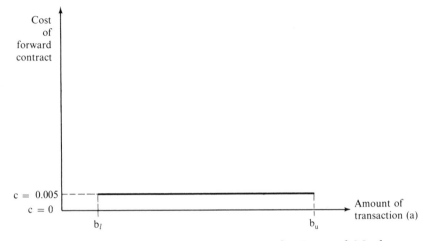

Figure 5. *Transaction Cost of Hedging in the Forward Market*

foreign exchange dealer to do large transactions in several chunks so that he avoids moving the price of the foreign currency. In terms of the amount of the transaction, the cost of a forward cover can be represented by a flat line at level 0.5% (see Figure 5), where:

c = effective cost of a forward cover;

b_l, b_u = lower and upper bounds on the transaction amount; i.e.,

$a < b_l$ | no forward contract
$a > b_u$ | is principally possible.

With respect to hedging in the money market, a distinction has to be made between borrowing (or investing) on the local money market and borrowing in the Euro-currency market. For example, borrowing French francs at the Credit Lyonnais in France versus borrowing Euro-French francs at FNCB in New York. In the case of local borrowing the foreign exchange loan is handled as any ordinary loan; consequently, the interest cost is an increasing step function of the amount borrowed with an upper limit representing the maximum amount the bank is willing to lend to a particular customer in a particular currency. As a result, the real cost of hedging in the local money market is equal to transaction cost (0.63%) plus the additional interest costs charged for amounts above the maximum of the line of credit (see Figure 6).

40

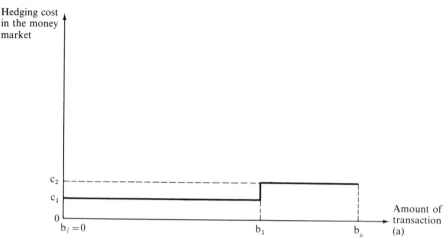

Figure 6. *Transaction and Additional Interest Costs of Hedging in the Local Money Market*

where:
b_l = lower bound = zero
b_1 = maximum amount of unused portion of line of credit
b_u = upper bound on loans in the currency and to the company in case
c_1 = hedging cost = transaction costs, for $0 < a \leq b_1$
c_2 = hedging cost = transaction costs + additional interest costs, for $b_1 < a \leq b_2$.

It was not possible to obtain from any of the bank officers a set of cutoff points for this step function for any currency or type of customer. The simple reason is that these cutoff points (b_i's) are a function of the customer, the currency, and even the timing of the transaction. For example, additional local borrowing or trade credit may be difficult or uneconomical to obtain, especially just before a major change in the exchange rate. The supplementary interest rate at b_1, i.e., $(i_2 - i_1)$, is usually of the order of 0.5% to 1%.

Although, theoretically, it is possible to extend the line of credit for hedging purposes at the cost of a slightly higher interest rate, this will seldom happen in practice. The overdraft facility is a major source of short-term financing for most companies. Because foreign

41

exchange loans are treated as any ordinary loan and use up the line of credit and in order to leave sufficient flexibility for local financing for other than foreign exchange reasons, it is a general practice to use the outstanding overdraft lines only for a certain maximum amount for exposure hedging (e.g., max. 75%). Only in cases of foreign exchange crises will the local line of credit be fully used or exceeded for pure hedging purposes.

Some companies are able to obtain, through the Euro-currency market, credit for hedging purposes in domestic currency that otherwise would have been unavailable to them at any price because of central bank credit rationing. The Euro-dollar market dominates by its overwhelming size the conditions in the remaining Euro-currency markets. A recent study by Marston [58] provides statistical evidence that Euro-currency rates are linked to the Euro-dollar rate through arbitrage operations undertaken by banks. The Euro-currency banks engage in extensive arbitrage operations which keep the non-dollar Euro-currency rates strictly in line. These banks are willing to accept deposits (and extend loans) in any currency which has an active forward market because they can always swap[2] the funds into dollars or into whatever other currency is in demand at the moment. Because of the continuing swapping between deposits among Euro-currency banks, Euro-currency rates are maintained at parity[3] regardless of the supply or demand pressures in any particular Euro-currency market. This was overwhelmingly evidenced by Marston's results of weekly and monthly estimation for the Euro-PS, Euro-DM, and Euro-SF rates. The banks interviewed said that in determining the rate of a Euro-currency loan, the loan officer calls the foreign exchange department of the bank and asks for the forward discount (or premium) and adds this to the Euro-dollar rate. This means that the rate of a Euro-currency loan equals

---

2. Put simply, the swap market provides an easy vehicle for a dealer to sell currency A against currency B for settlement on some future date and a counterbalancing purchase of currency A against currency B for settlement on another future date.

3. The Euro-currency rates are said to be at interest parity if the return on Euro-dollar deposits $(1 + i_{E\$})$ is equal to the covered return on Euro-currency deposits $(1 + i_{Ei}) \times {}_0 s_{1,i}/s_{0,i}$ (i = foreign currency).

the sum of the Euro-dollar loan rate plus the spread between forward and spot rates.

The Currency of the Hedging Transaction

A distinction has to be made between currencies traded in active exchange markets (e.g., most European currencies, $, C$, Yen, etc.) and those for which the market is thin or sometimes even non-existing (e.g., A$, DK, NK, SK, SAR, Mexican peso, Brazilian cruzeiro, Turkish lira, etc.). A currency is called "thin" or "odd" when it is traded in a market that is characterized by a small or limited supply and/or government imposed foreign exchange controls. Thin markets are usually also characterized by wide spreads and substantial price fluctuations during short time periods, since thinner markets do not have the capacity to absorb pressure and currency fluctuations. The main issue here is that aside from foreign exchange controls, the supply of the currency is permanently small;[4] the demand may vary. This creates an extra risk for the foreign exchange (or loan) officer, because it is much harder for him to make an offsetting deal in the same "exotic" currency. Compensation for this additional risk will usually result in a higher spread between the ask and bid prices quoted by the foreign exchange dealer and similarly to a higher differential between lending and borrowing rates charged by the loan officer. This risk premium or spread will be higher the larger the amount of the transaction, since it is harder to close a deal in a thin currency the larger the deal and simply because increasing demand pushes the price up. However, we like to distinguish three kinds of so-called "thin" currencies.

---

4. The supply of heavily traded currencies can also be small, but this can only be temporarily due to special circumstances. For example: (a) excessive speculative strains on a particular currency causing large changes in the exchange rates might limit the supply of the currency until the market eases and the rate is back to a "normal" level; (b) the exchange market in the US is broader in the morning when all foreign exchange markets in Europe are also open, than say at noon. So, the time of the day might have a determining impact on the supply of foreign funds; and (c) the supply of non-standard maturities (i.e., other than 1, 2, 3, 6, or 12 months) is much smaller. Consequently, closing a contract before maturity or entering a contract for an odd maturity can cause extra costs.

First, there are those currencies whose supply is limited but free of exchange controls (e.g., A$, DK, NK, etc.). For this category of thin currencies Interest Rate Parity holds since the absence of exchange controls does not interfere with the arbitrage equilibrating process between the money and foreign exchange markets. Hence, under the assumption of controlfree interest rates and no predictable exchange market intervention by central banks, the costs of hedging are zero. The cost functions specified earlier remain valid here.

Secondly, trading in some currencies is restricted by foreign exchange controls imposed by the local government (e.g., Mexican peso, Iranian rial). Interest parity does no longer hold for this second category of thin currencies because foreign exchange controls prohibit the international arbitrage process that keeps foreign exchange and money markets in equilibrium. For example, on 18 November 1976 the bid-ask spread for the Mexican peso was $24.5—$25.0 spot and $26.5 and $27.5 one month forward. The Mexican peso was thus selling at a 97.6% (i.e., 26.5 − 24.5/24.5 × 12 × 100) discount versus the US dollar. It is obvious that the difference between the US and Mexican interest rates was less than 97.6% (i.e., the borrowing rate in Mexico at that time was 28% while 6.25% in the US). The situation provided a unique opportunity to make a quick and substantial profit by borrowing Mexican pesos and at the same time buying them forward (at a 98% discount) to repay the loan. However, that is excluded in practice because the Mexican government did not allow any local borrowings except when there was a firm commercial contractual commitment expressed and payable (or receivable) in a foreign currency. The Mexican government was stabilizing spot rates but letting forward rates go free; speculation here clearly could destroy Interest Parity.

Under these conditions, the rate of exchange is completely determined by the forces of supply and demand, within the limits of foreign exchange controls. The conditions for Interest Parity are not satisfied. Hedging costs are non-zero and correspond to the deviation from the Interest Parity line. The cost functions are similar to the ones derived above, but with the first step being non-zero, representing the costs due to the inefficiency of the markets.

Finally, there is also a set of foreign currencies for which no forward exchange markets exists, i.e., a forward market may be prohibited by the foreign central bank. For example, there is no forward market in South African rands, Brazilian cruzeiros, Argentine pesos, Turkish liras, Chilian pesos, etc.). In this case the best alternative is hedging via a third currency. It is occasionally possible to hedge an exposure in a currency with no forward market by hedging in another currency that is likely to move against the US dollar by about the same amount as the first currency. The technique is often referred to as "parallel hedging".

Another alternative is local borrowing. This option will often be restricted by strict local government and exchange control regulations, such as: local borrowing might only be allowed if it is justified by commercial transactions; foreign exchange controls might prohibit local borrowings to leave the country (i.e., inconvertibility of the loan into another currency); compensating balance requirements imposed by local banks; or the payment of interests at the initiation of the loan (e.g., in Brazil). All these special restrictions make the effective interest rate much higher than the nominal rate of the loan. When the funds borrowed locally cannot leave the country or are not convertible into another (stronger) currency, the hedging transaction cannot be attractive to the firm since the high local interest rates cannot be offset by the investment rate on the funds converted into a strong currency.

Chapter VI

Taxation of Foreign Exchange
Gains and Losses

Hedging policies should aim at reducing after-tax exposure. Only after-tax costs are relevant to the hedging decision.

There exists a rule of thumb in the US saying that a forward foreign exchange contract equal to the exposure offsets the foreign position exactly before tax, and must be doubled in order to hedge the foreign exchange exposure after-tax. As with most folklore it is not totally inaccurate.

The recent literature on taxation of foreign exchange exposure[1] does not give a clear and definite answer to the international company's money manager. Even tax experts disagree on certain aspects of these problems because there is little by way of tax law and regulations. Neither courts nor administrators have developed a rational set of rules to account for exchange rate variations. The complexities of the tax problems are, of course, beyond the scope of this study. But most of the confusion in the matter of foreign currency re-valuation can be eliminated keeping in mind the following three principles:

—Tax authorities usually tax neither unrealized gains nor losses. This means that upon consolidation of balance sheet accounts, following FASB rules for reasons of public reporting, the exchange gains resulting from the translation of the consolidated foreign balance sheets are not taxable and so are the exchange losses not deductible for tax purposes. The reasoning is that exchange gains (or losses) due to translation of balance sheet accounts into a common

---

1. The interested reader is referred to the following publications: Blank [10], Chown, Kelen and Marcheal [14], Curtiss [15], Duncan [17], Ravenscroft [68], Ring [70].

base currency have no direct tax effects since these exchange gains (losses) are reported solely for bookkeeping purposes, but do not tell much about the economic situation of the firm. In fact, these gains and losses never (i.e., until dividends are paid or the subsidiary is sold or liquidated) produce actual currency conversions, but they do involve booking of gains and losses which the company must record regulary as foreign exchange gains and losses.

—When a company engages in hedging transactions to hedge expected exchange losses upon translation of its balance sheet accounts, exchange gains resulting from those hedging transactions are counted as ordinary income and hence are subject to corporate income taxes. Therefore, assuming t_i is the corporate tax rate for country i, the firm must cover $(1/1 - t_i)$ times the amount of the exposed position if it wants its net earnings after-tax to be unaffected by the change in the rates of exchange. This rule is essentially related to all balance sheet accounts, exception made for those accounts translated at historic rates (see Appendix I) and the A/R and A/P accounts which can be classified as operating transactions or cash flow generating elements of the balance sheet (see third principal). For those accounts, for example hedging outstanding long-term debt, no actual delivery of funds needs take place at maturity date of the forward contract. The company is hedging balance sheet positions rather than actual transactions, so it may buy the foreign currency spot at delivery date of the forward contract.

—Foreign exchange contracts which are integral and usual components of a company's international business, for example hedging outstanding A/R or A/P have no tax burden on the realized exchange gains and losses. In such cases, the forward contracts are self-liquidating, i.e., the company does not have to buy (or sell) the foreign currency spot at maturity date of the forward contract. As an example, hedging IL accounts receivable by selling IL forward for the amount and time period of the A/R outstanding. At the forward contract's maturity date, A/R collection is used to provide the IL to be exchanged for $ at the contractual forward rate. Hence, in general, forward contracts involving the transfer of funds in the normal cause of business do not incur the extra tax burden; i.e., there is no necessity for grossing-up the amount of the hedge.

Foreign Exchange Taxation and the "Expected Value-Variance" Relationship of the Foreign Currency Portfolio

With regard to the derivation of the relationship between the end-of-period expected value of the company's foreign exchange portfolio and its variance, as discussed in chapter VII, next follows proof that the tax system for exchange gains (losses) is irrelevant with respect to the shape of this frontier. In other words, the actual amount of hedging is a function of foreign exchange taxation, but the [expected value-variance] relationship for the foreign exchange portfolio is not.

We now specify this frontier under three different hypotheses of taxation, i.e., zero taxes, symmetrical taxes, and asymmetrical taxation of exchange gains (losses) resulting from hedging translation and transaction exposure. For reasons of simplification, it is assumed that all hedging is done in the forward exchange market. The following general notation is used:

X = exposure
h = amount of exposure hedged
Δ = transaction costs
t = tax rate
${}_0 s_1$ = forward exchange rate
$\tilde{s}_1$ = future spot rate at end of planning period
$\tilde{V}$ = value of the foreign exchange portfolio at end of the planning period

The Zero Tax Case

$$\tilde{V}(h_I) = X \times \tilde{s}_1 + h_I({}_0 s_1 - \tilde{s}_1 - \Delta)$$

$$\tilde{V}(h_I) = h_I \times {}_0 s_1 + (X - h_I) \times \tilde{s}_1 - \Delta \times h_I$$

$$\bar{V}(h_I) = h_I \times {}_0 s_1 + (X - h_I) \times \bar{s}_1 - \Delta \times h_I$$

$$\bar{V}(h_I) = h_I \times ({}_0 s_1 - \Delta) + (X - h_I) \times \bar{s}_1$$

$$\sigma_{\tilde{V}(h_I)} = (X - h_I)\sigma_{\tilde{s}_1}$$

or,

$$\bar{V}(h_I) = h_I \times ({}_0 s_1 - \Delta) + \frac{\bar{s}_1}{\sigma_{\tilde{s}_1}} \times \sigma_{\tilde{V}(h_I)} \qquad (1)$$

The relationship between $\bar{V}(h_I)$ and $\sigma_{\bar{V}(h_I)}$ is now derived for three different amounts of hedging, and is represented in Figure 7.

h_I	$\sigma_{\bar{V}(h_I)}$	$\bar{V}(h_I)$
0	$X \times \sigma_{\tilde{s}_1}$	$X \times \bar{s}_1$
$\frac{1}{2}X$	$\frac{1}{2} \times X \times \sigma_{\tilde{s}_1}$	$\frac{1}{2} \times X \times \left({}_0 s_1 - \Delta\right) + \frac{1}{2} \times X \times \bar{s}_1$
X	0	$X \times \left({}_0 s_1 - \Delta\right)$

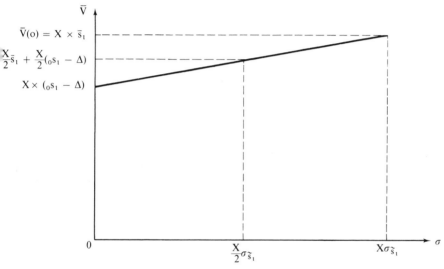

Figure 7. *Expected Value-variance Relationship*

Symmetrical Taxes on Both Translation and Transaction Exposure[2]

$$\tilde{V}(h_{II}) = X \times \tilde{s}_1 + (1 - t) \times h_{II} \times \left({}_0 s_1 - \tilde{s}_1 - \Delta\right)$$
$$\tilde{V}(h_{II}) = (1 - t) \times h_{II} \times {}_0 s_1 + \left(X - (1 - t) \times h_{II}\right)$$
$$\times \tilde{s}_I - (1 - t) \times h_{II} \times \Delta$$

---

2. In this context of taxes on foreign exchange gains (losses) translation and transaction exposure are defined as under principles two and three respectively (see p. 47).

$$\bar{V}(h_{II}) = (1 - t) \times h_{II} \times {}_0s_1 + (X - (1 - t) \times h_{II})$$
$$\times \bar{s}_1 - (1 - t) \times h_{II} \times \Delta$$
$$\sigma_{\bar{V}(h_{II})} = [X - (1 - t) \times h_{II}] \times \sigma_{\tilde{s}_1}$$

or,

$$\bar{V}(h_{II}) = (1 - t) \times h_{II}({}_0s_1 - \Delta) + \frac{\bar{s}_1}{\sigma_{\tilde{s}_1}} \times \sigma_{\bar{V}(h_{II})} \qquad (2)$$

Relation (2) equals (1), where

$$h_{II} = \frac{h_I}{1 - t} \qquad (3)$$

Substitution of (3) in (2):

$$\bar{V}\left(\frac{h_I}{1 - t}\right) = (1 - t) \times \frac{h_I}{(1 - t)} \times ({}_0s_1 - \Delta) + \frac{\bar{s}_1}{\sigma_{\tilde{s}_1}} \times \sigma_{\tilde{V}}$$

The same frontier is obtained as under the zero tax case, but with

$$h_{III} = \frac{h_I}{(1 - t)}.$$

Asymmetrical Taxes on Translation and Transaction Exposure

Let,

TL_1 = translation exposure hedged, $0 \leq TL_1 \leq TL$,

$\qquad TL$ is the maximum translation exposure

TX = transaction exposure

$h_{III} = TX + TL_1$

$X = TX + TL$

$$\tilde{V}(h_{III}) = X \times \tilde{s}_1 + TX({}_0s_1 - \tilde{s}_1 - \Delta) + (1 - t) \times TL_1$$
$$\times ({}_0s_1 - \tilde{s}_1 - \Delta)$$

or,

$$\tilde{V}(h_{III}) = [TX + (1 - t) \times TL_1] \times {}_0s_1 + [X - TX - (1 - t) \\
\times TL_1] \times \tilde{s}_1 - [TX + (1 - t) \times TL_1] \times \Delta$$

$$\bar{V}(h_{III}) = [TX + (1 - t) \times TL_1] \times {}_0s_1 + [X - TX - (1 - t) \\
\times TL_1] \times \bar{s}_1 - [TX + (1 - t) \times TL_1] \times \Delta$$

$$\sigma_{\bar{V}} = [X - TX - (1 - t) \times TL_1] \times \sigma_{\tilde{s}_1}$$

In comparison with the zero tax case a distinction has to be made between two separate cases:

A. If $h_I \le TX$

This means all net exposure is transaction exposure. Then,

$$\tilde{V}(h_{III}) = X \times \tilde{s}_1 + h_{III} \times ({}_0s_1 - \tilde{s}_1 - \Delta)$$

$$\tilde{V}(h_{III}) = (X - h_{III}) \times \tilde{s}_1 + h_{III}({}_0s_1 - \Delta)$$

$$\bar{V}(h_{III}) = (X - h_{III}) \times \bar{s}_1 + h_{III}({}_0s_1 - \Delta)$$

$$\sigma_{\bar{V}(h_{III})} = (X - h_{III}) \times \sigma_{\tilde{s}_1}$$

or,

$$\bar{V}(h_{III}) = h_{III}({}_0s_1 - \Delta) + \frac{\bar{s}_1}{\sigma_{\tilde{s}_1}} \times \sigma_{\bar{V}} \tag{4}$$

expression (4) equals (1), with $h_{III} = h_I$.

B. If $h_I > TX$

Total net exposure consists of translation exposure (TL_1) in addition to transaction exposure (TX), i.e.,

$$h_{III} = TX + TL_1.$$

$$\tilde{V}(h_{III}) = X \times \tilde{s}_1 + TX \times ({}_0s_1 - \tilde{s}_1 - \Delta) + (1 - t) \\
\times TL_1 \times ({}_0s_1 - \tilde{s}_1 - \Delta)$$

$$\tilde{V}(h_{III}) = [X - TX - (1 - t) \times TL_1]\tilde{s}_1 \\
+ [TX + (1 - t)TL_1]({}_0s_1 - \Delta)$$

$$\bar{V}(h_{III}) = [X - TX - (1 - t) \times TL_1]\bar{s}_1$$
$$+ [TX + (1 - t)TL_1](_0 s_1 - \Delta)$$
$$\sigma_{\bar{V}(h_{III})} = [X - TX - (1 - t) \times TL_1] \times \sigma_{\bar{s}_1}$$

or,

$$\bar{V}(h_{III}) = [TX + (1 - t)TL_1] \times (_0 s_1 - \Delta) + \frac{\bar{s}_1}{\sigma_{\bar{s}_1}} \times \sigma_{\bar{V}} \qquad (5)$$

To compare (5) to (1), let:

$$h_{III} = TX + (1 - t) \times TL_1 = h_{III, TX} + (1 - t)h_{III, TL_1}$$
$$h_I = TX + TL_1 = h_{I, TX} + h_{I, TL_1}$$

Expression (1) can now be rewritten as:

$$\bar{V}(h_I) = [h_{I, TX} + h_{I, TL_1}] \times (_0 s_1 - \Delta) + \frac{\bar{s}_1}{\sigma_{\bar{s}_1}} \times \sigma_{\bar{V}}$$

and (5) is now:

$$\bar{V}(h_{III}) = [h_{III, TX} + (1 - t) \times h_{III, TL_1}]$$
$$\times (_0 s_1 - \Delta) + \frac{\bar{s}_1}{\sigma_{\bar{s}_1}} \times \sigma_{\bar{V}}$$

Comparing the latter two equations, the case of asymmetrical taxation can be reduced to the zero tax case, when

$$h_{III, TX} = h_{I, TX} = TX$$

and

$$(1 - t) \times h_{III, TL_1} = h_{I, TL_1} \qquad \text{or} \qquad h_{III, TL_1} = \frac{h_{I, TL_1}}{(1 - t)}.$$

Example

An example follows to illustrate how different tax treatments of foreign exchange transactions influence the actual amounts of hedging but not the shape of the $\bar{V}(h) - \check{V}(h)$ frontier.

52

Consider the two currency portfolio:

Currency	A	B
Original exposure	$X(A) = \$ 10{,}000$	$X(B) = \$ 20{,}000$
Spot rate	$s_{0,\,A} = 0.0596$	$s_{0,\,B} = 1.0864$
Forward rate	$_0s_{1,\,A} = 0.0589$	$_0s_{1,\,B} = 1.0523$
Expected future spot rate (based on the Interest Rate Parity theorem)	$\bar{s}_{1,\,A} = 0.058905$	$\bar{s}_{1,\,B} = 1.049279$

Assume hedging to be restricted to the forward exchange market. The pure transaction costs are 0.5% of the transaction amount, $\Delta(A) = \Delta(B) = 0.005$. The total hedging costs per unit of foreign currency A and B is 0.000303 and 0.00241 respectively (i.e., total cost of hedging in \$ terms is $(\bar{s}_1 - {}_0s_1 + \Delta \times s_0)$ (for derivation see next chapter).

The covariance matrix for both currencies is:

	A	B
A	8.84E-4	2.40E-4
B	2.40E-4	13.08E-4

Zero taxes

The maximum (zero hedge) variance of the two currency foreign exchange portfolio is calculated as follows:

$$[10{,}000 \quad 20{,}000] \begin{bmatrix} 8.84E\text{-}4 & 2.40E\text{-}4 \\ 2.40E\text{-}4 & 13.08E\text{-}4 \end{bmatrix} \begin{bmatrix} 10{,}000 \\ 20{,}000 \end{bmatrix}$$

$$\Rightarrow \check{V} = 707{,}600, \ \sigma_{\tilde{p}} = 841.2$$

The corresponding (maximum) expected value of the portfolio is: $\$ 10{,}000 + \$ 20{,}000 = \$ 30{,}000$.

The table below summarizes some points of the frontier which is represented in Figure 8.

Amount hedged A	B	Total hedging costs	$\bar{V}(h)$	$\check{V}(h)(\times 10^3)$
0	0	0	$ 30,000	707.6
0	5,000	11.5	$ 29,988	454.7
9,000	10,000	69.3	$ 29,931	136.5
10,000	15,000	86.0	$ 29,914	32.7
10,000	20,000	97.4	$ 29,902	0

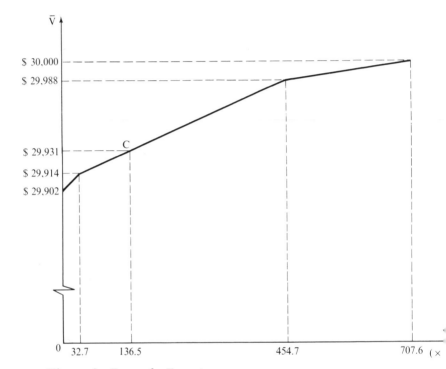

Figure 8. *Example Frontier*

Consider combination C, i.e., hedging 90% of the exposure in A and 50% of the exposure in currency B, to illustrate the formulas derived above.

In this case,

$h_{I, A} = 152,788$ or $9,000

$h_{I, B} = 9,530$ or $10,000,

54

and

$$\bar{V}(h_{I,A}; h_{I,B}) = \$\,29{,}931$$
$$\check{V}(h_{I,A}; h_{I,B}) = \$\,136{,}500.$$

Symmetrical taxation

For simplicity, assume currency A represents all translation exposure and B is transaction exposure. The corporate tax rate is supposed to be 50%. To obtain point C on the frontier would require hedging transactions with before-tax amounts equal to:

$$h_{II,A} = \frac{152{,}788}{0.5} = 305{,}576 \text{ or } \$\,18{,}000.$$

$$h_{II,B} = \frac{9{,}530}{0.5} = 19{,}060 \text{ or } \$\,20{,}000.$$

Under these tax rules:

$$
\begin{aligned}
\bar{V}(h_{II,A}; h_{II,B}) =\ & (1-t)[h_{II,A} \times {}_0s_{1,A} + h_{II,B} \times {}_0s_{1,B}] \\
& + [X(A) - (1-t)h_{II,A}] \times \bar{s}_{1,A} \\
& + [X(B) - (1-t)h_{II,B}] \times \bar{s}_{1,B} \\
& - (1-t) \times \Delta(A) \times h_{II,A} \times s_{0,A} \\
& - (1-t) \times \Delta(B) \times h_{II,B} \times s_{0,B}
\end{aligned}
$$

and

$$
\begin{aligned}
\check{V}(h_{II,A}; h_{II,B}) =\ & [\bar{s}_{1,A}(X(A) - (1-t) \times h_{II,A})]^2 \times \check{s}_{1,A} \\
& + [\bar{s}_{1,B}(X(B) - (1-t) \times h_{II,B})]^2 \times \check{s}_{1,B} \\
& + 2[\bar{s}_{1,A}(X(A) - (1-t)h_{II,A})] \\
& \times [\bar{s}_{1,B}(X(B) - (1-t)h_{II,B})] \times \mathrm{cov}(\tilde{s}_{1,A}; \tilde{s}_{1,B})
\end{aligned}
$$

or,

$$
\begin{aligned}
\bar{V}(305{,}576; 19{,}060) =\ & 0.5[17{,}998 + 20{,}057] + 1000 \\
& + 11{,}000 - 45.5 - 51.7 = 29{,}931 \\
\check{V}(305{,}576; 19{,}060) =\ & 884.03 + 130{,}800 + 4{,}800.2 \\
& = 136{,}484 = 136.5E3
\end{aligned}
$$

Similar computations could be made for all points on the frontier; which illustrates that the frontier remains the same, but the amounts of the hedging transactions have to be grossed up for the tax impact.

Asymmetrical taxation

At C, total amount of hedging consists of both transaction ($9,000 worth of A) and transaction exposure ($10,000 worth of B). The actual amount of hedging to be done to attain point C on the frontier is:

$$h_{III, A} = \frac{152,788}{0.5} = 305,576 \text{ or } \$18,000$$

$$h_{III, B} = 9,530 \text{ or } \$10,000.$$

Now,

$$\begin{aligned}
\bar{V}(h_{III, A}; h_{III, B}) = &(1 - t)h_{III, A} \times {}_0 s_{1, A} \\
&+ h_{III, B} \times {}_0 s_{1, B} \\
&+ [X(A) - (1 - t)h_{III, A}] \times \bar{s}_{1, A} \\
&+ [X(B) - h_{III, B}] \times \bar{s}_{1, B} \\
&- (1 - t) \times \Delta(A)h_{III, A} \times s_{0, A} \\
&- \Delta(B) \times h_{III, B} \times s_{0, B}
\end{aligned}$$

and,

$$\begin{aligned}
\check{V}(h_{III, A}; h_{III, B}) = &[\bar{s}_{1, A}(X(A) - (1 - t)h_{III, A}]^2 \times \check{s}_{1, A} \\
&+ [\bar{s}_{1, B}(X(B) - h_{III, B})]^2 \times \check{s}_{1, B} \\
&+ 2 \times \bar{s}_{1, A}[X(A) - (1 - t)h_{III, A}] \\
&\times \bar{s}_{1, B}[X(B) - h_{III, B}] \times \text{cov}(\tilde{s}_{1, A}; \tilde{s}_{1, B})
\end{aligned}$$

or,

$$\bar{V}(305,576; 9,530) = 0.5(17,999.4) + 10,028.4 + 1,000 + 10,000$$
$$- 45.5 - 51.7 = 29,931$$

and,

$$\check{V}(305,576; 9,530) = 136.5E3$$

56

Again, this demonstrates that the frontier remains unchanged but that in this case the hedging of translation exposure has to be grossed up by the tax impact.

It has been shown that the $(\bar{V} - \check{V})$ relationship is not affected by the method of taxation of exchange gains (losses), but that the actual amount of hedging is a function of the taxes. Therefore, in the next chapter we derive the portfolio model under the assumption of zero taxes.

Chapter VII

Portfolio Model for Foreign Exchange Exposure Management

The objective of the international company's foreign exchange management is to protect the company and its subsidiaries against exchange losses, but not to seek windfall gains through currency speculation or similar hedging activities unrelated to the nature of its business. The company's profitability should be based on the return on the goods and services it produces and sells, not on the return of its currency portfolio. Buying or selling currencies forward beyond the exposed position is speculation; so is taking open positions in currencies which can be covered at zero (ex-ante) costs. Protection against currency risk is the objective, not speculative profits.

The following notation will be used in the formulation of the model:

$\tilde{V}_1 =$ Value of the firm at the end of the period

$X_i =$ Projected local currency denominated exposure in currency i at the end of the period

$i =$ Subscript denoting the currencies in which the firm is conducting its business; i.e., $i = 1, 2, \ldots, N$; with $i = 1$ denoting the base currency of the company which is assumed to be the US dollar.

In order to be able to make a distinction between long and short positions in different currency exposures, the following conventional notation is introduced:

$i =$	1,	2, 3, ..., n;	n + 1, n + 2, ..., N
	base currency	currencies in which the company has a *long* exposure	currencies in which the company has a *short* exposure

58

$s_{0,i}$ = Spot rate for currency i; $i = 2, \dots, N$.

$\tilde{s}_{1,i}$ = Future spot rate for currency i; $i = 2, \dots, N$.

$_0 s_{1,i}$ = Forward exchange rate for currency i; $i = 2, \dots, N$.

$h_{1,i}$ = Amount of exposure in currency i hedged in *the forward market*; $i = 2, \dots, N$.

$h_{2,i}$ = Amount of exposure in currency i hedged in *the Euro-currency market*; $i = 2, \dots, N$.

$h_{3,i}$ = Amount of exposure in currency i hedged in *the local money market*; $i = 2, \dots, N$.

$[b_{l,1,i}; b_{u,1,i}]$ = Lower and upper bounds of hedging transactions in the forward market for currency i

$[b_{l,2,i}; b_{u,2,i}]$ = Lower and upper bounds of hedging transactions in the Euro-currency market for currency i

$[0; b_{u,3,i}]$ = Lower and upper bounds of hedging transactions in the local money market for currency i

TC = Transaction costs per unit amount of hedging (i.e., brokerage fees, information costs and administrative costs)

TC_1 = Unit TC in the forward market, expressed as a percentage of the hedging volume

TC_2 = Unit TC in the Euro-currency market, expressed as a percentage of the hedging volume

TC_3 = Unit TC in the local money market, expressed as a percentage of the hedging volume.

NOTE: It is assumed that all hedging transactions are taken at the beginning of the period. It is also assumed that there are no odd-day forward contracts and that all contracts are held to maturity.

r_i = Euro-currency interest rate for currency i; $i = 1, 2, \dots, N$ with r_1 = Euro-dollar interest rate

R_i = Local money market interest rate for currency i; $i = 1, 2, \dots, N$; with R_1 = US interest rate

Mathematical Derivation of the Model

To illustrate the derivation of the model, the three hedging alternatives will be considered consecutively and this for only *one* foreign currency (e.g., DM). Hence, X denotes the exposure in DM and it is assumed that $X > 0$.

The end-of-the-period value of the firm (ignoring its domestic US $ value) is the: $\tilde{V}_1 = X \times \tilde{s}_1$.

Hedging in the Forward Market:

$$\tilde{V}_1(h_1) = X\tilde{s}_1 + (h_1 \times {}_0s_1 - h_1 \times \tilde{s}_1 - h_1 \times TC_1 \times s_0)$$
$$= X\tilde{s}_1 + h_1({}_0s_1 - \tilde{s}_1 - TC_1 \times s_0)$$

Hedging in the Euro-currency Market:

Hedging a *long position* in a foreign currency consists of borrowing the foreign currency, converting these funds into the base currency ($) and investing them in the money market at the going rate (i.e., T-bill rate).

$$\tilde{V}_1(h_2) = X \times \tilde{s}_1 + [h_2 \times s_0(1 + r_\$) - h_2 \times (1 + r_{DM})\tilde{s}_1$$
$$- h_2 \times TC_2 \times s_0]$$
$$= X \times \tilde{s}_1 + h_2[s_0 \times (1 + r_\$)$$
$$- (1 + r_{DM}) \times \tilde{s}_1 - TC_2 \times s_0]$$

Similarly, hedging *a short position* in a foreign currency consists of borrowing the base currency ($), converting it into local currency and investing the proceeds in the money market. Hence,

$$\tilde{V}_1(h_2) = X\tilde{s}_1 + [h_2 \times s_0(1 + r_{DM}) - h_2(1 + r_\$)\tilde{s}_1$$
$$- h_2 \times TC_2 \times s_0]$$
$$= X\tilde{s}_1 + h_2[s_0(1 + r_{DM}) - \tilde{s}_1(1 + r_\$) - TC_2 \times s_0]$$

Assuming the long DM-exposure X can be covered by both hedging alternatives simultaneously, then:

60

$$\tilde{V}_1(h_1, h_2) = [X - h_1 - (1 + r_{DM}) \times h_2] \times \tilde{s}_1 + h_1 \times {}_0 s_1 + h_2$$
$$\times (1 + r_\$) - h_1 \times TC_1 \times s_0 - h_2 \times TC_2 \times s_0.$$

Hedging in the Local Money Market:

The procedure is exactly similar to hedging in the Euro-currency market; only the notation changes; i.e., $h_3, R_\$, R_{DM}, TC_3$ instead of $h_2, r_\$, r_{DM}$ and TC_2.

The $\tilde{V}_1$ function is:

$$\tilde{V}_1(h_3) = X \times \tilde{s}_1$$
$$+ [h_3 \times s_0 \times (1 + R_{DM}) - h_3 \times (1 + R_\$)$$
$$\times \tilde{s}_1 - h_3 \times TC_3 \times s_0]$$
$$= X \times \tilde{s}_1 + h_3[s_0(1 + R_{DM}) - \tilde{s}_1(1 + R_\$) - TC_3 \times s_0]$$

Considering the three hedging alternatives simultaneously:

$$\tilde{V}_1(h_1, h_2, h_3) = [X - h_1 - (1 + r_{DM}) \times h_2 - (1 + R_{DM}) \times h_3]$$
$$\times \tilde{s}_1 + h_1 \times {}_0 s_1 + (1 + r_\$) \times h_2 \times s_0$$
$$+ (1 + R_\$) \times h_3 \times s_0 - h_1 \times TC_1 \times s_0 - h_2$$
$$\times TC_2 \times s_0 - h_3 \times TC_3 \times s_0.$$

grouping of the terms with respect to the decision variables (h_1, h_2, h_3):

$$\tilde{V}_1(h_1, h_2, h_3) = X \times \tilde{s}_1 - h_1 \times [\tilde{s}_1 - {}_0 s_1 + TC_1 \times s_0] - h_2$$
$$\times [(1 + r_{DM})\tilde{s}_1 - (1 + r_\$)s_0 + TC_2 \times s_0] - h_3$$
$$\times [(1 + R_{DM})\tilde{s}_1 - (1 + R_\$)s_0 + TC_3 \times s_0]$$

the expected value of $V_1(h_1, h_2, h_3)$ is:

$$\bar{V}_1(h_1, h_2, h_3) = X \times \bar{s}_1 - h_1 \times [\bar{s}_1 - {}_0 s_1 + TC_1 \times s_0] - h_2$$
$$\times [(1 + r_{DM})\bar{s}_1 - (1 + r_\$)s_0 + TC_2 \times s_0] - h_3$$
$$\times [(1 + R_{DM})\bar{s}_1 - (1 + R_\$)s_0 + TC_3 \times s_0]$$

61

The variance of $V_1(h_1, h_2, h_3)$ is:

$$\check{V}_1(h_1, h_2, h_3) = [X - h_1 - (1 + r_{DM})h_2 - (1 + R_{DM})h_3]^2 \times \check{s}_1$$

Under the assumption of efficient markets and zero transaction costs, however,
(a) $TC_1 = TC_2 = TC_3 = 0$
(b) $\bar{s}_1 = {}_0s_1$ (the forward rate is the unbiased forecast of the future spot rate)
(c) Interest Parity holds: $E(\tilde{s}_1) = \bar{s}_1 = s_0(1 + r_s/1 + r_{DM})$
$\Rightarrow \bar{s}_1(1 + r_{DM}) = s_0(1 + r_s)$
and analogously,

$$\bar{s}_1(1 + R_{DM}) = s_0(1 + R_s)$$

The "HEDGE" strategy leads to:

$$\tilde{V}_1(h_1, h_2, h_3) = X\tilde{s}_1$$
$$\bar{V}_1(h_1, h_2, h_3) = X\bar{s}_1 = X_0s_1$$
$$\check{V}_1(h_1, h_2, h_3) = [X - h_1 - (1 + r_{DM})h_2 - (1 + R_{DM})h_3]^2 \times \check{s}_1$$

The "NO HEDGE" strategy implies:

$$\tilde{V}_1(h_1, h_2, h_3) = X \times \tilde{s}_1$$
$$\bar{V}_1(h_1, h_2, h_3) = X \times {}_0s_1$$
$$\check{V}_1(h_1, h_2, h_3) = X^2 \times \check{s}_1$$

Comparing the "HEDGE" with the "NO HEDGE" policy under the assumption of efficient markets and zero transaction costs, it can be deduced that the right policy is to hedge all exposure all the time. The expected value of the firm is the same, but the variance of the firm's end-of-period value is reduced under the "HEDGE" strategy.

Next follows the generalized derivation of the model going from the one currency case to the N-currency case. The value of the

62

international company (only with regard to changes in foreign exchange rates) at the end of the period is then represented by:

$$\tilde{V}_1(h_1, h_2, h_3) = X_1 + \sum_{i=2}^{N} X_i \times \tilde{s}_{1,i}$$

$$- \sum_{i=2}^{N} h_{1,i}(\tilde{s}_{1,i} - {}_0 s_{1,i} + TC_1 \times s_{0,i})$$

$$- \sum_{i=2}^{n} h_{2,i}[(1 + r_i)\tilde{s}_{1,i} - (1 + r_1)s_{0,i} + TC_2 \times s_{0,i}]$$

$$- \sum_{i=n+1}^{N} h_{2,i}[(1 + r_1)\tilde{s}_{1,i} - (1 + r_i)s_{0,i} + TC_2 \times s_{0,i}]$$

$$- \sum_{i=2}^{n} h_{3,i}[(1 + R_i)\tilde{s}_{1,i} - (1 + R_1)s_{0,i} + TC_3 \times s_{0,i}]$$

$$- \sum_{i=n+1}^{N} h_{3,i}[(1 + R_1)\tilde{s}_{1,i} - (1 + R_i)s_{0,i} + TC_3 \times s_{0,i}]$$

The expected value of the company at the end of the period is:

$$\bar{V}_1(h_1, h_2, h_3) = X_1 + \sum_{i=2}^{N} X_i \times \bar{s}_{1,i}$$

$$- \sum_{i=2}^{N} h_{1,i}(\bar{s}_{1,i} - {}_0 s_{1,i} + TC_1 \times s_{0,i})$$

$$- \sum_{i=2}^{n} h_{2,i}[(1 + r_i)\bar{s}_{1,i} - (1 + r_1)s_{0,i} + TC_2 \times s_{0,i}]$$

$$- \sum_{i=n+1}^{N} h_{2,i}[(1 + r_1)\bar{s}_{1,i} - (1 + r_i)s_{0,i} + TC_2 \times s_{0,i}]$$

$$- \sum_{i=2}^{n} h_{3,i}[(1 + R_i)\bar{s}_{1,i} - (1 + R_1)s_{0,i} + TC_3 \times s_{0,i}]$$

$$- \sum_{i=n+1}^{N} h_{3,i}[(1 + R_1)\bar{s}_{1,i} - (1 + R_i)s_{0,i} + TC_3 \times s_{0,i}]$$

The variance of the $\tilde{V}$-value is:

$$\check{V}_1(h_1, h_2, h_3)$$

$$= \sum_{i=2}^{n} \sum_{j=2}^{n} \bar{s}_{1,i}[X_i - h_{1,i} - (1 + r_i)h_{2,i} - (1 + R_i)h_{3,i}]$$

$$\times \bar{s}_{1,j}[X_j - h_{1,j} - (1 + r_j)h_{2,j} - (1 + R_j)h_{3,j}] \times \text{cov}(\tilde{s}_{1,i}, \tilde{s}_{1,j})$$

$$+ \sum_{i=n+1}^{N} \sum_{j=n+1}^{N} \bar{s}_{1,i}[X_i - h_{1,i} - (1 + r_1)h_{2,i} - (1 + R_1)h_{3,i}]$$

$$\times \bar{s}_{1,j}[X_j - h_{1,j} - (1 + r_1)h_{2,j} - (1 + R_1)h_{3,j}] \times \text{cov}(\tilde{s}_{1,i}, \tilde{s}_{1,j})$$

$$+ 2 \sum_{i=2}^{n} \sum_{j=n+1}^{N} \bar{s}_{1,i}[X_i - h_{1,i} - (1 + r_i)h_{2,i} - (1 + R_i)h_{3,i}]$$

$$\times \bar{s}_{1,j}[X_j - h_{1,j} - (1 + r_1)h_{2,j} - (1 + R_1)h_{3,j}] \times \text{cov}(\tilde{s}_{1,i}, \tilde{s}_{1,j})$$

NOTE: Every component of the above expression is pre-multiplied by the forecasted future spot exchange rate, because the foreign currency exposure (X_i) and the decision variables $(h_{1,i}, h_{2,i}, h_{3,i})$ are expressed in foreign currency.

Under Efficient Market Conditions and Zero Transaction Costs, however:

(a) $TC_1 = TC_2 = TC_3 = 0$

(b) $\bar{s}_{1,i} = {}_0 s_{1,i} \; \forall \; i$

(c) $\begin{cases} s_{0,i}(1 + r_1) = \bar{s}_{1,i}(1 + r_i) \\ s_{0,i}(1 + R_1) = \bar{s}_{1,i}(1 + R_i) \; \forall \; i \end{cases}$

(d) $\begin{cases} s_{0,i}(1 + r_i) = \bar{s}_{1,i}(1 + r_1) \\ s_{0,i}(1 + R_i) = \bar{s}_{1,i}(1 + R_1) \; \forall \; i \end{cases}$

The " HEDGE" strategy implies:

$$\tilde{V}_1(h_1, h_2, h_3) = X_1 + \sum_{i=2}^{N} X_i \tilde{s}_{1,i}$$

$$\bar{V}_1(h_1, h_2, h_3) = X_1 + \sum_{i=2}^{N} X_i {}_0 s_{1,i}$$

$$\check{V}_1(h_1, h_2, h_3) = \text{see expression above.}$$

Under the assumption of efficient markets and no transaction costs, ex-ante costs of hedging are zero, i.e., one can reduce the variance $\check{V}$ to zero at no costs. However, ex-post hedging costs might differ from zero, but will still be relatively small since deviations occur on both sides of the Interest Parity line. In practice, transaction costs are also non-zero. Figure 9 represents the relation between the expected value of the firm and the variance of this value for both ex-ante and ex-post hedging costs under the efficient market hypothesis.

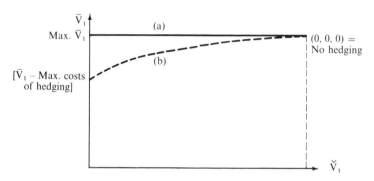

Figure 9. (a) *Ex-ante Costs of Hedging and Zero Transaction Costs*
(b) *Ex-post Costs of Hedging and Positive Transaction Costs*

The " NO HEDGE" strategy implies:

$$\tilde{V}_1(0, 0, 0) = X_1 + \sum_{i=2}^{N} X_i \tilde{s}_{1,i}$$

$$\bar{V}_1(0, 0, 0) = X_1 + \sum_{i=2}^{N} X_{i\,0} s_{1,i}$$

$$\check{V}_1(0, 0, 0) = \sum_{i=2}^{N} \sum_{j=2}^{N} X_i \times {}_0 s_{1,i} \times X_j \times {}_0 s_{1,j}$$

$$\times \operatorname{cov}(\tilde{s}_{1,i}; \tilde{s}_{1,j})$$

Hence, under the efficient market hypothesis and no transaction costs, the recommended strategy is to hedge all exposed currency

65

positions, because compared with the "no hedge" strategy, the variance of the value of the firm at the end of the period is lower while the expected value remains unchanged.

Final Version of the Foreign Exchange Portfolio Model

Since the model is directed to the minimization of the foreign exchange risk to the company, the portfolio is restricted to the foreign currencies in which the company is exposed (i.e., leaving out the $ denominated assets and liabilities, X_1). Applying standard portfolio theory, the quadratic algorithm iteratively minimizes the quadratic objective function $\breve{V}_1(h_1, h_2, h_3)$ subject to different values of a linear constraint $\bar{V}_1(h_1, h_2, h_3)$. However, two additional sets of linear constraints are introduced:

(a) the first set of constraints represents the lower and upper bounds on the amount of hedging transactions for the three methods of hedging, i.e.,

—forward market

$$b_{l, 1, i} \leq h_{1, i} \leq \text{Min}[b_{u, 1, i}; X_i]; \forall i$$

—Euro-currency market

$$b_{l, 2, i} \leq h_{2, i} \leq \text{Min}[b_{u, 2, i}; X_i]; \forall i$$

—local money market

$$0 \leq h_{3, i} \leq \text{Min}[b_{u, 3, i}; X_i]; \forall i$$

For every currency, the upper bound is the minimum of the regular upper limit valid per hedging alternative and the original exposure in the particular currency. This is to avoid speculation, i.e., undertaking a hedging transaction for an amount larger than the one exposed.

(b) The second set of constraints states that, although any currency exposure can be hedged making use of more than one hedging technique, total amount hedged per currency must be less than the original exposure in that currency, i.e.,

$$0 \leq h_{1, i} + h_{2, i} + h_{3, i} \leq X_i; \forall i$$

66

The mathematical formulation of the final portfolio model is then:

Min $\check{V}_1(h_1, h_2, h_3)$

$$= \underset{h_{1,i},\, h_{2,i},\, h_{3,i}}{\text{Min}} \sum_{i=2}^{n} \sum_{j=2}^{n} \bar{s}_{1,i}[X_i - h_{1,i} - (1 + r_i)h_{2,i} - (1 + R_i)h_{3,i}]$$

$$\times \bar{s}_{1,j}[X_j - h_{1,j} - (1 + r_j)h_{2,j} - (1 + R_j)h_{3,j}] \times \text{cov}(\tilde{s}_{1,i}, \tilde{s}_{1,j})$$

$$+ \sum_{i=n+1}^{N} \sum_{j=n+1}^{N} \bar{s}_{1,i}[X_i - h_{1,i} - (1 + r_i)h_{2,i} - (1 + R_1)h_{3,i}]$$

$$\times \bar{s}_{1,j}[X_j - h_{1,j} - (1 + r_1)h_{2,j} - (1 + R_1)h_{3,j}] \times \text{cov}(\tilde{s}_{1,i}, \tilde{s}_{1,j})$$

$$+ 2 \sum_{i=2}^{n} \sum_{j=n+1}^{N} \bar{s}_{1,i}[X_i - h_{1,i} - (1 + r_i)h_{2,i} - (1 + R_i)h_{3,i}]$$

$$\times \bar{s}_{1,j}[X_j - h_{1,j} - (1 + r_1)h_{2,j} - (1 + R_1)h_{3,j}] \times \text{cov}(\tilde{s}_{1,i}, \tilde{s}_{1,j})$$

subject to:

(1) $b_{l,1,i} \leq h_{1,i} \leq \text{Min}[b_{u,1,i}; X_i]; \forall\, i$

(2) $b_{l,2,i} \leq h_{2,i} \leq \text{Min}[b_{u,2,i}; X_i]; \forall\, i$

(3) $0 \leq h_{3,i} \leq \text{Min}[b_{u,3,i}; X_i]; \forall\, i$

(4) $0 \leq h_{1,i} + h_{2,i} + h_{3,i} \leq X_i; \forall\, i$

(5) $\displaystyle\sum_{i=2}^{N} X_i \times \bar{s}_{1,i} - \sum_{i=2}^{N} h_{1,i}(\bar{s}_{1,i} - {}_0 s_{1,i} + TC_1 \times s_{0,i})$

$$- \sum_{i=2}^{n} h_{2,i}[(1 + r_i)\bar{s}_{1,i} - (1 + r_1)s_{0,i} + TC_2 \times s_{0,i}]$$

$$- \sum_{i=n+1}^{N} h_{2,i}[(1 + r_1)\bar{s}_{1,i} - (1 + r_i)s_{0,i} + TC_2 \times s_{0,i}]$$

$$- \sum_{i=2}^{n} h_{3,i}[(1 + R_i)\bar{s}_{1,i} - (1 + R_1)s_{0,i} + TC_3 \times s_{0,i}]$$

$$- \sum_{i=n+1}^{N} h_{3,i}[(1 + R_1)\bar{s}_{1,i} - (1 + R_i)s_{0,i} + TC_3 \times s_{0,i}]$$

$$= K$$

Chapter VIII

Field Research on the Current Practice of Exposure Management

To acquire a better understanding of actual foreign exchange problems and current business practices, the author studied the foreign exchange exposure management in fourteen US multi-national companies. The companies interviewed are not listed for reasons of confidentiality. They are all in the Fortune's Directory of the largest US industrial companies.

The results of extensive interviews with the money managers of these companies are summarized below in a series of separate issues.

Definition of Foreign Exchange Exposure

All companies interviewed define their net foreign exchange exposure in accordance with the FASB No. 8 principles. In addition to the accounting exposure they also consider transaction exposure which is usually based on a cash forecast received monthly (or quarterly) from their subsidiaries. In other words, economic exposure is used as the basis for exposure management. For one company only accounting exposure was definitely much more important than its transaction exposure. The explanation is simple, the company's foreign operating subsidiaries manufacture and sell their products in the local markets, i.e., cash in- and outflows offset each other largely in the local currencies.

In three other cases, accounting exposure is never part of effective exposure management because of its relative insignificance. Transaction exposure only is considered for exposure management by two of these companies since their overseas operating subsidiaries do not manufacture but only distribute the parent company's products abroad. The exposure of the foreign subsidiaries equals sales abroad which are expressed in local currency. The third company does not manufacture a series of standardized products, but instead works on a contract basis, mostly of a long-term nature and often government sponsored. However, all transaction exposure is covered on the forward exchange market for each contract separately and the hedging costs are built in the sales price.

Organization of Exposure Management

There are several arguments in favor of a central control and direction of foreign exchange management, such as netting out currency positions among subsidiaries to reduce float in the system, avoidance of double hedging of long and short positions in the same currency at different subsidiaries, preventing that the hedging efforts by one subsidiary uncover the foreign exchange exposure of another subsidiary, etc. Central control of foreign exchange management requires the availability of an adequate reporting system to gather and disseminate information throughout the organization.

In practice, there is often a lack of coordination of foreign exchange management among companies' subsidiaries and an absence of an adequate reporting system. Only ten out of the fourteen companies actually have a fully centralized system for foreign exchange exposure management. In addition, a number of them are still managing foreign exchange on the basis of incomplete and often delayed information.

In one company, each subsidiary is treated as a profit center that is also responsible for its own foreign exchange management. Headquarters may advise particular hedging transactions to its subsidiaries, but also these transactions will be executed at the selected subsidiary level. This implies that a subsidiary might have to take a loss, unrelated to its operations, for the sake of the overall well-being of the international group. A lack of coordination among subsidiaries can easily cause unnecessary and costly hedging transactions for offsetting foreign exchange positions between subsidiaries.

Another company has also organized its exposure management in a decentralized way with its subsidiaries acting as independent profit centers. The reason is that these foreign firms are in very diverse types of businesses and hard to integrate given their specific nature and requirements. On the basis of quarterly reports only transaction exposure is coordinated among the different subsidiaries. The idea is to have the subsidiaries as being self-liquidating, i.e., set up the financing of the local subsidiary in such a way that its income from operations match its financing requirements.

The other two companies only centralize accounting exposure management at corporate headquarters, leaving economic exposure to the best judgment of local management. This is again only defendable if subsidiaries sell to local markets only, if not, unnecessary covering transactions will be taken by the different subsidiaries separately due to neglecting the advantages resulting from offsetting cash flows in various subsidiaries expressed in the same currency.

The companies interviewed varied strongly from very passive to very active exposure management. One company prepares an annual budget on the basis of four quarterly financial exposure forecasts, then it determines an acceptable risk level for the current year (i.e., maximum exchange loss that could be taken considering the impact on the end-of-year earnings per share). The exposure management then simply consists of doing nothing, except for hedging all potential losses from exchange exposure above the budgeted maximum level of exposure. In contrast with this very conservative type of exposure management, another company centralizes its world-wide transaction exposure on a day-to-day basis via a Swiss-based concentration bank.[1] Every morning the treasurer receives a telex from the concentration bank specifying the amount of cash available or needed per currency. On the basis of internal assessments and Reuterpress instant currency quotations he decides in what currencies and for which periods to invest, to cover or not cover the net exposure in particular currencies, etc. This transaction exposure is supplemented with balance sheet exposure management based on monthly reports and weekly telex updates.

---

1. A concentration bank is the bank where the company keeps most of its deposits and consequently centralizes most of its operations.

70

Complete centralization of foreign exchange exposure management does not necessarily imply an efficient management. This was clearly the case in one company which organized its exposure management on a country by country basis, requiring a monthly report of economic exposure from each subsidiary. These monthly statements must, however, be completely translated in the local currency. Headquarters considered the net exposure of each subsidiary as the company's exposure in the local currency, i.e., the French subsidiary translates all its balance sheet accounts and their respective forecasts into French francs, the net exposure of the French subsidiary is then considered to be the French franc exposure of the company. It is obvious that such a system contains a real danger of overhedging. For example, the French subsidiary buys most of its raw materials from West-Germany, while the Dutch subsidiary sells a lot of its products in Germany. For consolidation purposes, the DM accounts payable to the French subsidiary are translated into French francs, as the DM export receipts of the Dutch subsidiary are converted into guilders. The company followed the policy of hedging only down-side risk and leaving upvaluation-prone positions unhedged. Hence, they might consider to hedge the French franc long position only. In fact, no hedging transactions were needed if consolidation would be done on a currency basis instead of by country, because the long and short DM positions might to a large extent balance each other out.

The overall objective of exchange exposure management put forward by the companies was the minimization of exchange risk and its impact on the company's financial statements, certainly not the maximization of profits on their currency portfolio. Two companies admitted that they would also take on commercially justified currency positions from time to time to benefit from estimated changes in particular exchange rates. All companies strongly opposed outright speculation in the foreign exchange market, i.e., any position taken in a particular currency must be justified by its commercial transactions.

The time horizon of exposure management was overwhelmingly one quarter. Exposure forecasts are made on a quarterly basis up to one year ahead. In some companies transaction exposure on large sales contracts is hedged on an individual basis.

Assessment of Exchange Rate Changes

Very few international companies make any serious effort to fore-cast exchange rates, despite the huge risks that potential changes in exchange rates carry. In fact, in all fourteen companies but two, nobody is in charge of making currency forecasts. The main reason is the feeling that it is too difficult to forecast exchange rate move-ments, or that exchange rate forecasts are too inaccurate to be worth the cost. The treasurer's assessments are completely judgmental using outside information gathered through staff reports, articles in newspapers and magazines, official statistics and mostly talks with knowledgeable people such as bankers and economists. The set of factors referred to by the money managers in making currency predictions is listed below:

(a)   comparative inflation rates;
(b)   balance of payments accounts (i.e., trade balance, current balance, basic balance, international reserves);
(c)   money supply (M_1);
(d)   unit labor costs;
(e)   national income;
(f)   industrial production;
(g)   unemployment;
(h)   interest rate differentials;
(i)   forward markets (premiums/discounts);
(j)   political situation (national monetary and fiscal policy, politi-cal stability);
(k)   international currency agreements (e.g., the European "snake" agreement, the creation of a European monetary union based on the ECU);
(l)   historical performance of currencies;
(m)   stock market indices.

It is important to emphasize that not all these factors are considered to be relevant at all times. Besides, estimates of these factors must be available on time and be believed by everyone to be of any value in predicting currency behavior.

Methods of Hedging

Several hedging techniques are available to the international company. Most companies ranked first the adjustment of intracompany payments via " leads and lags ", i.e., speeding up or prepayment of funds due from a subsidiary operating in a weak currency country or the slowing of payments from strong currency subsidiaries, and the related techniques of adjustment of transfer prices. One company used local borrowing most heavily to hedge its foreign exchange exposure for the good reason that its subsidiaries produce and sell in the same country (i.e., total production = local sales). Local borrowings are used for two main purposes: to provide working capital in the local currency; and for conversion into a hard currency in order to speed up such hard currency payables as dividends, royalties and imports, and to provide intracompany loans. Local borrowing was mostly used to a maximum extent by the company to offset long positions in the local currencies and consequently to reduce net financial exposure to almost zero. There are, however, limits to this strategy such as the requirement that the funds borrowed locally must be convertible into US dollars (e.g., the Banque de France does not allow the transfer of locally borrowed funds into dollars).

Especially the companies which operate on a contract basis often incorporate a price adjustment formula (escalation clause) in their sales contracts with customers. Such a built-in currency clause may specify that any exchange gains or losses are for the customer's account, so that the company receives a fixed dollar equivalent for its contract. If this is not acceptable to the customer, one might consider the inclusion of a trading band (e.g., a 2% band) within which the exchange rate may fluctuate without causing a renegotiation of the sales contract price, the eventual loss or gain is for the company or the customer. Or if a change in the exchange rate exceeds this band, then the agreement says that the exchange gain (loss) will be shared between the company and its customer. In these companies, hedging of transaction exposure is done on a project by project basis. The selection of the escalation clause to take care of the volatility of exchange rate changes is negotiated with the customer in setting up the sales contract.

Similarly, in those cases where the company has a dominant position (price leader) in its market segment, regular price adjustments can to a large extent take care of balance sheet exposure. The final outcome is obviously largely dependent on the relative bargaining position of the company and its customer, the competitive strength of the company and the existence of price controls imposed by local governments.

The forward exchange market was often ranked last as a refuge against exchange losses, because it was mostly considered to be an expensive method of hedging (i.e., most businessmen defined the cost of a forward cover wrongly as the spread between the spot and forward exchange rates), and because of the omnipresence of uncertainty about future spot rates. Another problem is that long term sales contracts are hard to cover because such forward exchange contracts exist for most major trading currencies only for terms up to twelve months.

Hedging Practices

Although the business executives interviewed almost universally deny any attempt to speculate on currency fluctuations, some corporate hedging practices seem to include an element of speculation. The general practice of all companies interviewed except for one is to hedge only down-side risk and never hedge long positions in upvaluation-prone currencies. For example, assuming the company's consolidated balance sheet shows accounts receivables in roughly equal dollar-equivalent amounts in a strong and a weak currency, e.g., DM and IL. All companies reported that they would consider covering the lira exposure but never the DM exposure. No company would consider locking in a potential exchange gain buying the DM forward; nor would they think of the inverse co-movement (negative correlation) between expected changes in the DM and IL rates which could imply that no covering has to be done at all. They argued not to speculate on currency movements since they would not consider buying more DM than the amount already exposed, i.e., all exposure should be commercially justified.

All companies responded alike confronted with an illustrative problem of establishing a subsidiary in The Netherlands, financing plant and equipment completely by local borrowing, while its products are sold in the Netherlands. Assuming that the Guilder upvalues, would you hedge potential exchange loss on the long-term exposure in Guilders? Not one company claimed to hedge the long-term debt outstanding. The reasons being that the dollar value of servicing the long-term debt will be offset by the dollar value of the income stream from local sales.

Confronted with the question "Should the corporation risk cash by hedging to protect a purely accounting (non-cash related) exposure?" most financial executives were reluctant to risk cash to defend a purely accounting exposure unless the magnitude of the exposure is sufficient to pose a threat to the stability of corporate earnings. When faced with an exposure of this magnitude, the prudent corporation will take protective action unless the cost of protection outweighs the risk associated with the exposure.

Only one company hedged all its exposure consistently. All others hedged selectively making a trade-off between hedging costs and reduction of exchange risk. Most argued that consistent hedging is too expensive. This is a logical consequence of considering the spread between forward and spot exchange rates as being the costs of hedging.

It is interesting to mention that not one company would either hedge in other currencies than the ones they are doing business in, i.e., covering their risks by hedging in a third currency that has a large market and may be expected to move in the same direction as the currency of the original transaction (this is often called parallel hedging); or balancing out exposure on a global or multi-currency basis, i.e., for example, offsetting a long position in DM with a short position in DG, or a long position in IL. All hedging transactions are made on a currency by currency analysis never considering, let alone, exploiting the statistical relationship (correlation) between different currencies.

Summary of Major Findings

The field research showed that a number of international companies are still (a) managing foreign exchange on the basis of incomplete and delayed information; (b) dealing with exposure management on a currency by currency basis, i.e., failing to recognize the statistical relationship between the currencies in its foreign exchange portfolio; (c) restricting hedging to the covering of positions which seem to contain downside risk and leaving uncovered foreign exchange positions which seem to contain upside potential; and (d) defining the costs of hedging as the spread between spot and forward rates.

Chapter IX

Practical Implementation of the Model in a Corporate Environment

The model developed in the previous chapter has been applied to a US multinational firm. For reasons of confidentiality, however, the firm will be called the "Exa" Company.

Exa designs, manufactures, sells and services highly sophisticated expensive equipment. The company currently operates fourteen manufacturing plants throughout the world. The products of the overseas manufacturing subsidiaries in most instances are sold to the company's foreign sales subsidiaries or the parent corporation and other foreign manufacturing subsidiaries for further processing. All its domestic and foreign subsidiaries are wholly-owned. Exa's products are used world-wide in a wide variety of applications. Over the years, Exa has built a world-wide customer support and service system. The company has over 5,000 professionals deployed throughout the large number of sales offices to provide service and technical support to the growing customer base.

Sales and marketing operations outside the United States are conducted principally through sales subsidiaries abroad, by direct sales from the parent company and, to a lesser extent, through various representative and distributorship arrangements. A substantial portion of these sales consists of products manufactured domestically. Sales outside the US represented thirty-eight percent of total operating revenues for the year 1976.

Exa is primarily equity financed; it is a blue chip on the New York Stock Exchange. The company's sales are expected to grow at about thirty percent per annum over the next few years.

The company is the dominating firm and price leader in its specific segment of its industry. This allows the company to adjust prices regularly. As a matter of fact, prices are set quarterly. New price books are printed every three months. For example, on 15 December of each year, the company sets new prices for its products, then it takes a few days to print and send the new price books to all its subsidiaries, but from 1 January on, the new price book is in use in every subsidiary for the following three months. The procedure for drafting a new price list starts with the specification of all prices in US dollars, then one adds to this first a "business uplift", specified as a percentage surcharge reflecting the local inflation rate plus freight and duty costs, and a "hedge cost" uplift. For example, if the discount on the Norwegian krone is $2\frac{3}{4}$ percent, one might put in a one percent "hedge cost" surcharge. The resulting prices determine the US dollar-value of overseas sales. Spot rates are then used to convert the US dollar price book into local currency price books. The so-called business uplift takes care to a large extent of eventual exposure losses by adjusting local prices for the differential in relative inflation rates. With the exception of eventual price controls in particular countries, Purchasing Power Parity should partially hold for Exa, and exchange gains and losses should balance out, at least to some extent. In fact, one could make the argument that no hedging operations need be taken, as the company is automatically hedged by means of its price adjustment facility. However, Exa still has an uncertainty problem, in response to the variation of the value of the firm around its mean.

Foreign exchange exposure management for all Exa's subsidiaries is centralized at corporate headquarters in the USA. Balance sheets and cash flow statements are sent monthly by all subsidiaries to the international money manager in the US. Total consolidated corporate foreign exchange exposure is defined as the sum of three different elements: (a) balance sheet exposure as set forth by FASB No. 8; (b) "backlog", these are outstanding orders accepted at fixed prices in terms of foreign exchange; and (c) projected bookings, which are projected orders over the next quarter. The time period of its exposure managements is one quarter.

The main objective of foreign exchange exposure management at Exa is the protection of its earnings per share. The pricing policy takes care of the concern about keeping foreign exchange transactions from interfering with the steady stream of earnings per share as far as the mean value of the earnings is concerned. However, protection of the variance in earnings per share requires additional hedging. This latter issue is the basis for applying the portfolio model, i.e., making the appropriate selection of hedging transactions to reduce the variance of its foreign exchange portfolio to a reasonable level.

Moreover, exposure management is absolutely subordinated to the true business activities of the company, manufacturing and selling its product. This means, for example, that although foreign exchange management might require local borrowing, this will be subordinated to current needs for short-term financing of its day-to-day business operations.

Exa has two consultant banks on foreign exchange management. Both banks provide Exa's money manager weekly with an outlook for every currency in which the company is exposed (currency by currency) and on this basis they recommend hedging margins per currency. These hedging ratios are specified in steps of 20%; e.g., on the basis of the currency outlook we recommend you cover 20% FF, 60% of the IL, etc. . . . of your present position in the particular currency.

The Data Base for the Model

The data provided by Exa corporation are as of 31 December 1976. The consolidated foreign exchange exposure statement is summarized in Table 3 below.

Exa has lines of credit outstanding in every country which could be used for hedging purposes. However, those local credit lines are too small to account for all hedging operations. Besides, cash management is also centralized in the US. On Tuesday every subsidiary telexes the amount of excess cash it will transfer on the following Thursday; so that every Friday morning the total of company-wide excess funds are available for investment at company headquarters. No matter what happens on Tuesday and Wednesday, the subsidiaries transfer on Thursday the amount specified on Tuesday, if need be making use of the local overdraft line. For this purpose and also to leave sufficient flexibility for local financing for other than foreign exchange reasons, Exa adapts the general rule that the upper limit on local borrowing for hedging purposes is ninety percent of

Table 3. *Consolidated Exposure Statement (all in $)*

Currency	B/S Exposure	Backlog	Projected bookings	Total
AS	24,372	43,648	24,955	92,975
A$	3,639	5,914		9,553
BF	32,338	72,656	47,343	152,337
C$	15,097	41,569	26,556	83,222
DG	12,102	18,157	11,702	41,961
DK	2,552	9,044	7,552	19,148
DM	4,244	57,516	36,298	98,058
FF	7,851	56,795	26,317	90,963
IL	3,432,077	6,771,500	2,605,948	12,809,525
NK	1,035	10,706	3,712	15,453
PS	1,926	26,464	15,884	44,274
SF	5,232	14,021	14,840	34,093
SK	4,127	28,760	21,556	54,443
SP	51,643	63,408	144,095	259,146
Y	468,505	1,184,365		1,652,870

local lines of credit. The lower bound on hedging in the local money market is obviously zero. The local lines of credit are given in Table 4.

Hedging in the Euro-money market is limited to a few big currencies for Exa, i.e., DG, DM, FF, PS, and SF. Exa does not bother to enter the Euro-currency market for an amount less than $ 100,000 equivalent. The upper limit of transactions in the Euro-currency market is so high that it is not binding for the foreign currency exposures of the company. This implies that the upper bound on hedging in the Euro-currency market equals the total exposure for every currency. The Euro-rates are also listed in Table 4.

The forward market is also for Exa the preferred method of hedging out of the three methods considered here, for the same reasons as discussed in chapter V (pp. 31–32). The minimum amount of any hedging transactions in the forward market is considered to be $ 1,000,000 equivalent. The upper bound is the amount of exposure in every foreign currency. The amounts of foreign currency exposure of Exa are large enough to move the exchange rates (and consequently the costs of forward cover) if they were to be hedged

Table 4. *Input Data for the Model*

Currency	Spot exchange rate	Forward exchange rate*	Euro-currency rate*	Local money interest rate*	90% of line of credit (in $)
AS	0.0596	0.0589	—	7.25%	225,000
A$	1.0864	1.0523	—	9.75%	1,350,000
BF	0.0279	0.0267	—	11.25%	225,000
C$	0.9929	0.9832	—	7.5%	3,600,000
DG	0.4075	0.4017	6–4/8%	8.0%	1,440,000
DK	0.1728	0.1617	—	13.5%	27,000
DM	0.4133	0.4138	5–1/2%	7.0%	6,120,000
FF	0.2012	0.1924	11–1/2%	10.0%	1,620,000
IL	0.001148	0.00101	—	19.5%	1,980,000
NK	0.1929	0.1907	—	7.5%	18,000
PS	1.7102	1.5755	13–7/8%	15.5%	4,860,000
SF	0.4081	0.4091	4–7/16%	6.25%	2,070,000
SK	0.2463	0.2340	—	11.5%	630,000
SP	0.0146	0.0136	—	9.5%	333,000
Y	0.0035	0.00336	—	7.5%	1,440,000
$			5–1/8%	6.0%	

* All three months rates (as of 31 December 1976).

completely in the forward market at once. In order to avoid the danger of moving the price of the foreign currency, very large hedging transactions are executed in chunks spread over several days. Exa has excellent relations with the foreign exchange trading departments of its banks, its AAA rating allows an almost unrestricted flexibility to extend its lines of credit for foreign exchange trading purposes. In practice, all this means that the cost of hedging in the forward market as a function of the amount of the transaction can be represented as a flat line for Exa.

More relevant input data for the model are summarized in Table 4.

As mentioned above, Exa determines the $-equivalent of its total exposure by converting all local currency exposures at the current spot rate. Instead of this approach, the $-value of foreign exchange exposure will be evaluated by converting at the expected future spot

81

Table 5. *Translation (TL) and Transaction (TX) Exposure as Defined for Tax Purposes (all in $ terms)*

Currency	TL	TX	TL + TX
AS	− 1,400	6,877	5,477
A$	− 193	9,902	9,709
BF	− 299	4,495	4,196
C$	− 3,429	84,908	81,479
DG	− 275	17,039	16,782
DK	− 20	3,094	3,074
DM	− 4,719	47,424	42,705
FF	− 2,775	20,411	17,636
IL	− 837	13,880	13,043
NK	− 106	3,102	2,996
PS	− 9,843	79,334	69,491
SF	− 2,804	16,684	13,880
SK	− 277	13,880	13,603
SP	− 128	3,790	3,662
Y	− 1,776	8,144	6,368
			$\sum = \overline{304{,}101}$

rates, since the model considers the expected value of the firm at the end of the planning period, i.e., at the end of the next quarter. Therefore, the necessity to make an estimate of the spot rates for the currencies involved at the end of the first quarter of 1977. For this purpose, the forecasting model based on the Fisher theorem (see chapter IV, p. 23) has been used. The resulting expected spot rates $(\bar{s}_{1,i})$ are:

AS	0.058905	IL	0.0010182
A$	1.049279	NK	0.1902083
BF	0.0265833	PS	1.5695341
C$	0.9790455	SF	0.4071397
DG	0.3999537	SK	0.2341506
DK	0.1613814	SP	0.0141333
DM	0.4152587	Y	0.0034511
FF	0.1938836		

With regard to the discussion of the taxation of foreign exchange transactions, translation and transaction exposure are now defined

Table 6. *Expected Hedging Costs*

Currency	Forward Market Disequil. cost	Forward Market TRCST (%)	Euro-currency Market Disequil. cost	Euro-currency Market TRCST (%)	Local Money Market Disequil. cost	Local Money Market TRCST (%)
AS	0.000005	0.5	—	0.63	0	0.63
A$	−0.003021	0.5	—	0.63	0	0.63
BF	−0.0001167	0.5	—	0.63	0	0.63
C$	−0.004155	0.5	—	0.63	0	0.63
DG	−0.001746	0.5	−0.0024337	0.63	0	0.63
DK	−0.0003186	0.5	—	0.63	0	0.63
DM	0.0014587	0.5	0.0036163	0.63	0	0.63
FF	0.0014836	0.5	0.0046687	0.63	0	0.63
IL	0.0000082	0.5	—	0.63	0	0.63
NK	−0.0004917	0.5	—	0.63	0	0.63
PS	−0.005966	0.5	−0.010541	0.63	0	0.63
SF	−0.00196	0.5	−0.02944	0.63	0	0.63
SK	0.0001506	0.5	—	0.63	0	0.63
SP	0.0005333	0.5	—	0.63	0	0.63
Y	0.0000911	0.5	—	0.63	0	0.63

for tax purposes adding A/R to the company's "backlog" and "projected bookings" (see chapter VI) and also using the derived expected future spot rates. Table 5 shows that the resulting "net" exposure is a transaction exposure for every currency. This reduces Exa's foreign exchange problem to the case of asymmetrical taxes on translation and transaction exposure as discussed in chapter VI.

As has been discussed in chapter V, transaction costs are defined in accordance with the recent Frenkel and Levich study [28]. In the forward market, hedging consists of buying or selling foreign currency forward. Using the previous notation, transaction costs are thus, $TC_1 = t_f = 0.5\%$. Hedging a long position in the Euro-currency market consists of borrowing foreign currency, converting these funds into US dollars and investing them in interest bearing assets (e.g., US T-bills). Transaction costs are then, $TC_2 = t^* + t_s + t = 0.10\% + 0.50\% + 0.03\% = 0.63\%$. Or, for a short position, hedging involves the borrowing of US dollars, converting them into the foreign currency and invest these foreign funds for the borrowing period. Transaction costs incurred are $TC_2 = t + t_s + t^*$

$= 0.03\% + 0.5\% + 0.10\% = 0.63\%$. The transaction costs for hedging via the local money market are completely similar to those in the Euro-currency market, i.e., 0.63%, but the currency of the transaction is now local foreign currency instead of Euro-currency.

Table 6 summarizes the components of expected total hedging costs per method of hedging for every currency in the portfolio. Notice that the estimated disequilibrium costs for hedging in the money market are by definition zero, since the estimate of the future spot rate has been derived on the basis of the Fisher theorem.

The Quadratic Programming Model

The practical application of the model developed in chapter VII has been made possible by making use of a modified version of the quadratic programming model (QPLC) devised by Prof. J. Bishop of the Harvard Business School. This program can generally be used to solve optimization problems where the criterion is quadratic and the constraints linear. The original model has been adapted in a pure mathematical way to have zero lower bounds on all decision variables. This is easily achieved by defining the new decision variables as $\eta_{1,i} = h_{1,i} - b_{l,1,i}$; $\eta_{2,i} = h_{2,i} - b_{l,2,i}$; and $\eta_{3,i} = h_{3,i} - b_{l,3,i} = h_{3,i}$ as $b_{l,3,i} = 0$ for all i. The righthand sides of the constraints are now, for reasons of notational simplification, denoted as:

$$M_{1,i} = X_i - b_{l,1,i}$$

$$M_{2,i} = X_i - b_{l,2,i}$$

$$M_{3,i} = X_i - 0$$

$$G_i = X_i - b_{l,1,i} - (1 + r_i)b_{l,2,i}$$

The formulation of the model is further simplified by the fact that all Exa's foreign exchange exposures are net long positions. The model with all notational simplifications is then:

$$\text{Min} \sum_{i=1}^{15} \sum_{j=1}^{15} [\bar{s}_{1,i}(G_i - \eta_{1,i} - (1 + r_i)\eta_{2,i} - (1 + R_i)\eta_{3,i})]$$
$$\times [\bar{s}_{1,j}(G_j - \eta_{1,j} - (1 + r_j)\eta_{2,j}$$
$$- (1 + R_j)\eta_{3,j})] \times \text{cov}(\tilde{s}_i, \tilde{s}_j)$$

Subject to:

(1) $0 \le \eta_{1,i} \le M_{1,i}$

(2) $0 \le \eta_{2,i} \le M_{2,i}$

(3) $0 \le \eta_{3,i} \le M_{3,i}$

(4) $0 \le \eta_{1,i} + (1 + r_i)\eta_{2,i} + (1 + R_i)\eta_{3,i} \le G_i$

(5) $\displaystyle\sum_{i=1}^{15} X_i \bar{s}_{1,i} - \sum_{i=1}^{15} (\eta_{1,i} + b_{l,1,i})$

$$\times\, (\bar{s}_{1,i} - {}_0 s_{1,i} + TC_1 \times s_{0,i})$$

$$-\sum_{i=1}^{15} (\eta_{2,i} + b_{l,2,i}) \times [(1 + r_i)\bar{s}_{1,i} - (1 + r_{\$})s_{0,i}$$

$$+\, TC_2 \times s_{0,i}]$$

$$-\sum_{i=1}^{15} \eta_{3,i}[(1 + R_i)\bar{s}_{1,i} - (1 + R_{\$})s_{0,i} + TC_3 \times s_{0,i}] = K$$

The QPLC model specifies an "efficient frontier" between the variance of the company's currency portfolio and the expected value of this portfolio at the end of the three-month period. This frontier is derived by changing the righthand side of the single equality constraint, K', i.e.,

(5) can be rewritten as:

$$\sum_{i=1}^{15} (\bar{s}_{1,i} - {}_0 s_{1,i} + TC_1 \times s_{0,i})\eta_{1,i} + \sum_{i=1}^{15} [(1 + r_i)\bar{s}_{1,i}$$

$$-\, (1 + r_{\$})s_{0,i} + TC_2 \times s_{0,i}]\eta_{2,i} + \sum_{i=1}^{15} [(1 + R_i)\bar{s}_{1,i}$$

$$-\, (1 + R_{\$})s_{0,i} + TC_3 \times s_{0,i}]\eta_{3,i} = \sum_{i=1}^{15} X_i \bar{s}_{1,i} - \sum_{i=1}^{15}$$

$$\times\, (\bar{s}_{1,i} - {}_0 s_{1,i} + TC_1 \times s_{0,i})b_{l,1,i} - \sum_{i=1}^{15} [(1 + r_i)$$

$$\times\, \bar{s}_{1,i} - (1 + r_{\$})s_{0,i} + TC_2 \times s_{0,i}]b_{l,2,i} - K$$

$$=\text{Constant} - K = K'.$$

This modified equation sets total hedging costs equal to K'; so for different K'-values, starting from $K' = 0$, the model derives the corresponding $\check{V}$-value deriving in this way the "frontier" or [hedging costs $\Leftrightarrow$ reduction in $\check{V}$] trade-off function for the company. For every point of the frontier the program also determines the optimal mix of hedging activities, i.e., the currency positions to be hedged and the method of hedging to be used. In the Exa case, the foreign exchange portfolio consists of fifteen currencies; this implies forty-five decision variables (fifteen currencies × three alternative methods of hedging) and sixty-one constraints. A complete description of the portfolio model for Exa is given in Appendix IV. The $[\bar{V} \Leftrightarrow \check{V}]$ frontier has been derived under five different assumptions. Before discussing the results, remember that the company will have to take a foreign exchange loss (or profit), whether the company engages in hedging activities or not. The expected value of the foreign exchange loss (or profit) corresponds to the difference in value of the foreign currency portfolio valued at the current spot rates and the expected future spot rates at the end of the planning period. Exa will have to take an expected foreign exchange loss of \$ 11,649,750, i.e.,

$$\sum_{i=1}^{15} X_i \times s_{0,i} - \sum_{i=1}^{15} X_i \times \bar{s}_{1,i} = \$\,315{,}751{,}250 - \$\,304{,}101{,}500.$$

However, most of this foreign exchange loss has already been anticipated and recuperated by means of the price adjustments made for the first quarter of 1977.

The Results

The portfolio model has been applied to the Exa data under a set of varying assumptions. The results of the practical implementation of the model are summarized successively for the following cases, i.e., application to the original Exa data, assuming zero off-diagonal elements in the covariance matrix of exchange rates, ignoring transaction costs, defining costs of hedging incorrectly as the discount (premium) on the foreign currency, and finally allowing for cross-hedging.

The Original Data

The expected value of the company's foreign exchange portfolio at the end of the first quarter of 1977 is equal to $\sum_{i=1}^{15} X_i \bar{s}_{1,i} =$ $ 304,101,500. The corresponding maximum variance of the foreign exchange portfolio is 28×10^{12}, the standard deviation is thus 5.29×10^6. However, in terms of the computer model, maximum variance occurs when the amounts hedged are at their minimum levels, when $K' = 0$ (zero hedging costs) and $\eta_{1,i} = \eta_{2,i} = \eta_{3,i} = 0$ for $i = 1, 2, \ldots, 15$. But because of the redefinition of the decision variables (i.e., $\eta_i = h_i - b_{1,i}$); zero levels for all η_i's means hedging all currency positions at their respective lower bounds in the forward and Euro-currency market. The maximum variance of the portfolio corresponding to all $\eta_i = 0$, is 24×10^{12} ($\sigma_{\bar{v}} = 4.9 \times 10^6$). This also implies a total hedging cost of $ 130,600. Since this amount of hedging is imposed in an artificial way to satisfy the zero lower bounds on all decision variables in the QPLC program, all results are reported in terms of the outcome of the QPLC model, i.e., decision variables are the η_i's, max $\check{V} = \check{V}(0,0,0) = 24 \times 10^{12}$ and maximum $\bar{V} = \bar{V}(0, 0, 0) = $ 304,101,500 - $ 130,600 = $ 303,970,900.

Table 7. *Expected Value and Variance of the Foreign Exchange Portfolio for Different Amounts of Hedging (all in $)*

Hedging Costs	$\bar{V}$	$\check{V}(\times 10^{12})$
0	303,970,900	23.06
25,000	303,945,900	9.22
50,000	303,920,900	8.09
100,000	303,870,900	6.03
200,000	303,770,900	3.87
300,000	303,670,900	2.22
400,000	303,570,900	1.08
500,000	303,470,900	0.50
700,000	303,270,900	0.08
950,000	303,020,900	0.004
1,033,666	302,937,240	0.0

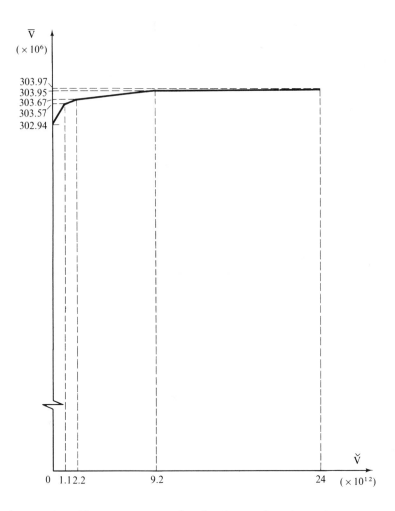

Figure 10. *Efficient Frontier for the Original Data*

The minimum variance occurs at maximum hedging, i.e., when $\eta_{1,i} + (1 + r_i)\eta_{2,i} + (1 + R_i)\eta_{3,i} = G_i$ for all i. Zero variance is obtainable in the Exa case, since the upper bounds on the amounts which can be hedged in any of the three methods of hedging are not restricting the satisfaction of the fourth set of constraints (i.e., $\eta_{1,i} + (1 + r_i)\eta_{2,i} + (1 + R_i)\eta_{3,i} \leq G_i$) for any of the fifteen currencies.

88

The expected value of Exa's foreign exchange portfolio in function of the variance of this value and the relationship between the reduction in portfolio variance in terms of total hedging costs incurred are depicted in Figures 10 and 11 respectively. The summary data for both relationships are the outcome of the QPLC program and are listed in Table 7 (p. 87).

The optimal mix of hedging transactions is simultaneously determined by the program for every point on the frontier. This selection is illustrated for the points *A*, *B* and *C* of the frontier (see Figure 11).

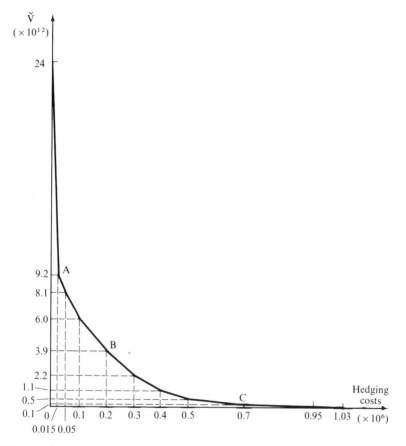

Figure 11. *Variance-hedging Costs Relationship for the Original Data*

A: Total hedging costs incurred: $25,000
Variance partially hedged portfolio: 9.22×10^{12}
Hedging activities:

| | | Amount Hedged | | |
Currency	Total exposure	Forward market	Euro-currency market	Local money market
BF	121,830	121,830		
C$	82,200	5,514		
DG	39,230		36,800	
PS	43,040	576	37,800	
SF	31,390	31,385		

B: Total hedging costs incurred: $200,000
Variance of partially hedged portfolio: 3.87×10^{12}
Hedging activities:

| | | Amount Hedged | | |
Currency	Total exposure	Forward market	Euro-currency market	Local money market
A$	8,380	8,333		
BF	121,830	121,830		
C$	82,200	82,200		
DG	39,230		36,800	
DK	13,210	13,210		
DM	100,190		31,000	
NK	10,570	10,570		
PS	43,040	576	37,800	
SF	31,390	31,390		

C: Total hedging costs incurred: $ 700,000
Variance of partially hedged portfolio: 0.08×10^{12}
Hedging activities:

| Currency | Total exposure | Amount Hedged | | Local money market |
		Forward market	Euro-currency market	
AS	76,220	76,200		
A$	8,380	8,330		
BF	121,830	121,830		
C$	82,200	82,200		
DG	39,230		36,800	
DK	13,210	13,210		
DM	100,190	425	94,600	
FF	85,440			8,050
IL	11,935,000	2,965,000		1,732,280
NK	10,570	10,570		
PS	43,040	575	37,800	
SF	31,390	31,390		
SK	53,970	53,970		
SP	190,654			22,810
Y	1,551,230			423,530

Figures 10 and 11 show that a full hedge (zero variance) strategy would involve $ 1,033,660 hedging costs. This is much less than a full hedge strategy would cost where hedging is limited to the forward market only; i.e., to reduce the variance to zero when all hedging is done in the forward exchange market would cost $ 1,342,481. Exa, as most companies interviewed, limited its hedging operations almost exclusively to the forward market, for the reasons discussed above in chapter V. The results demonstrate that important savings (e.g., $ 308,000 for Exa) could be made by incorporating the other two methods of hedging, and by hedging a particular currency exposure in more than one market.

The asymptotic behavior of the curve in Figure 11 at both ends of the axes, means that some currencies are very cheap to hedge while others are extremely expensive to cover. This implies that, even if only for theoretical purposes, one wants to reduce the portfolio's variance to zero, very high hedging costs will be incurred at the extreme lower end of the variance. In practice, the variance could be reduced to a very low level, say from 24 units to 0.5, at a total cost of $500,000. That is only 50% of the hedging costs associated with zero variance.

Zero Off-diagonal Elements in the Covariance Matrix of Exchange Rates

As mentioned before, foreign exchange exposure is managed by Exa on a currency by currency basis. This amounts to setting all $\text{cov}(\tilde{s}_i, \tilde{s}_j) = 0$ for all $i \neq j$ in the objective function. The resulting covariance matrix is diagonal. The resulting maximum variance of the firm's foreign exchange portfolio is now, by definition, smaller than in the previous case, i.e., $\check{V}_{max} = 6.87 \times 10^{12}$. After hedging all currency exposure to their lower bounds in every market ($\forall \eta_i = 0$) the variance is reduced to 6.08×10^{12} at a total cost of hedging equal to $130,600.

The summary data from which the frontier will be derived are given in Table 8:

Table 8. *Expected Value and Variance of the Foreign Exchange Portfolio for Different Amounts of Hedging (all in $)*

Hedging costs	$\bar{V}$	$\check{V}(\times 10^{12})$
0	303,970,900	6.08
20,000	303,950,900	2.95
50,000	303,920,900	2.5
100,000	303,870,900	2.0
300,000	303,670,900	0.62
600,000	303,370,900	0.12
1,033,660	302,937,240	0.0

It is obvious that setting all off-diagonal covariances equal to zero leads to a serious understatement of the true variance of the foreign exchange portfolio. The variance measured in the correct way is 24×10^{12}, while only 6×10^{12} when one ignores all covariances among the currencies in the portfolio.

92

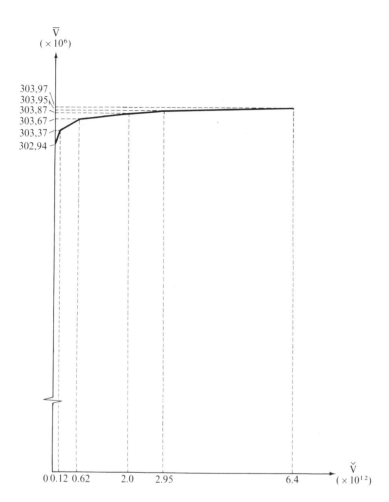

Figure 12. *Efficient Frontier*

It is interesting to compare how much risk is left after spending a certain amount of dollars on hedging costs under both assumptions, i.e., with zero and non-zero covariances in the objective function of the model. Therefore, the curves of Figures 12 and 13 are plotted in the same diagram; see Figure 14.

Figure 14 shows that for small amounts of hedging the understatement of the true variance of the foreign exchange portfolio is

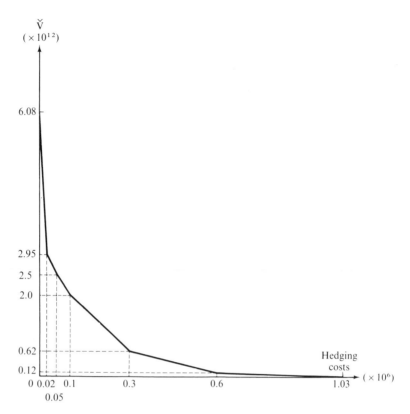

Figure 13. *Variance-hedging Costs Relationship*

considerable, while the discrepancy between both curves almost disappears at large amounts of hedging (i.e., for total costs of hedging over $ 500,000).

Zero Transaction Costs

Some of the international companies interviewed claimed that there are no transaction costs. The person(s) in charge of foreign exchange exposure management have many other tasks in the company. They are a sort of fixed cost to the company and do not represent a proportional cost to the hedging activity. Moreover, some of the foreign exchange traders also claimed that no brokerage fees are

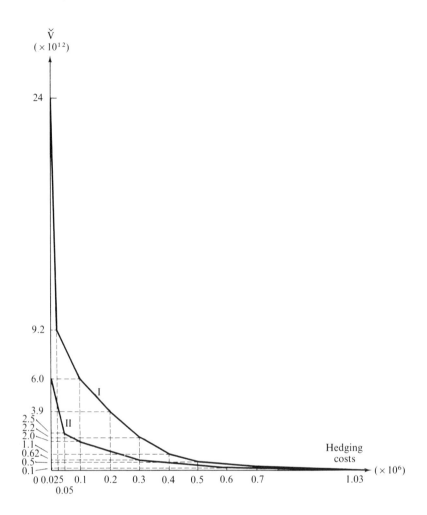

Figure 14. *Variance-hedging Costs Relationship for the Original Data (Curve I) and Zero Off-diagonal Covariance Matrix (Curve II) Cases*

95

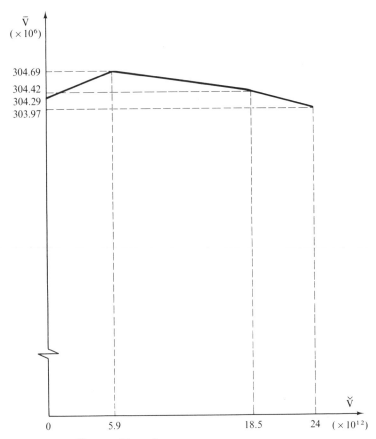

Figure 15. *Efficient Frontier*

charged for good customers, as hedging is only a minor part of the bank's business with the company.

However, the case of zero transaction costs fits for the analysis of incremental costs of hedging in the forward market with respect to the costs of transacting in the future spot market. Since the cost of transactions in spot exchange rates and forward exchange rates were defined to be equal (see chapter V), they can be ignored in comparing a forward cover with a transaction in the future spot market.

With $TC_1 = TC_2 = TC_3 = 0$, the real cost of hedging is negative for most currencies in Exa's portfolio. In fact, only ten out of the

96

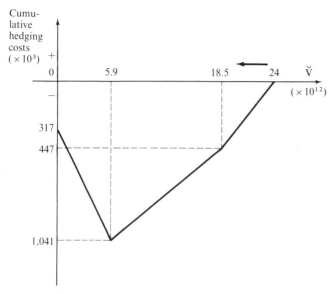

Figure 16. *Hedging Costs Versus Portfolio Variance*

forty-five decision variables, representing eight foreign currencies have positive hedging costs associated with them. Hence, the equality constraint (i.e., total hedging costs = K') is binding only up to a certain level of hedging costs. This maximum amount of positive hedging costs is $724,268. From that level on, all hedging costs are non-positive. This implies that the total foreign exchange exposure can be partially hedged at zero or negative costs. In such a situation where most unit hedging costs are negative, one could pursue a full hedge strategy and maximize expected foreign exchange gains. Full hedging under the assumption of zero transaction costs means a projected net foreign exchange profit of $317,558 for Exa.

If we make the rational assumption that in reducing the variance $\check{V}$ from its maximum value to zero, the company hedges first making use of those combinations of currencies and methods of hedging with a negative cost; then the $(\bar{V} - \check{V})$ frontier will first rise towards that point representing maximum expected gains from hedging. From there on, the curve will decline to its minimum value, i.e., at $\check{V} = 0$. This relationship and the variance-hedging costs trade-off are depicted in Figure 15 and Figure 16 respectively.

Still many companies consider the discount (premium) on a foreign currency as the real cost part of total hedging costs. In order to test this erroneous assumption the costs of hedging are set equal to the sum of the spread between the forward and spot exchange rates and transaction costs.

Under this assumption, it costs the company much more for hedging one dollar equivalent foreign exchange exposure than under the correct definition of hedging costs. The following table and Figures 17 and 18 illustrate this statement.

Table 9. *Expected Value and Variance of the Foreign Exchange Portfolio for Different Amounts of Hedging (all in \$)*

Hedging costs	$\bar{V}$	$\check{V}(\times 10^{12})$
0	303,970,900	23.96
1,000,000	303,970,900	7.10
2,000,000	301,970,900	5.66
4,000,000	299,970,900	3.36
6,000,000	297,970,900	1.62
8,000,000	295,970,900	0.53
10,000,000	293,970,900	0.11
11,663,657	292,307,243	0.0

The by definition much higher costs of hedging explain why some money managers claim that they cannot afford to hedge most of the company's foreign exchange exposure because it is too expensive. This results in several foreign exchange positions left unhedged; while the discount (or premium) on those foreign currencies will have to be taken by the company, whether those positions are hedged or not. Using the correct definition of hedging costs, as defined in chapter V, small hedging costs are an incentive to the company to fully hedge and lock in every potential foreign exchange loss (or gain) at a very low cost.

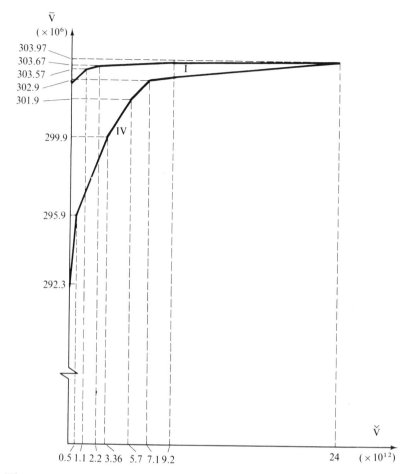

Figure 17. *Comparison of the Efficient Frontier (Curve IV) with the Original Data Case (Curve I)*

Cross-hedging

Although the covariances between different currencies were taken into consideration in all previous sections, except for one (p. 92), as opposed to the traditional foreign exchange management which determined the overall risk of the foreign exchange portfolio by adding the variances of the individual currencies in the portfolio,

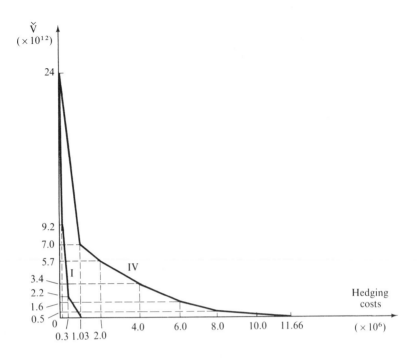

Figure 18. *Variance-hedging Costs Relationship for the Original Data (Curve I) and under Incorrect Definition of Hedging Costs (Curve IV)*

exposure management was basically still restricted to a currency by currency "hedge-no-hedge" decision problem. In all previous tests of the model, no allowance was made to engage in a hedging trans-action for an amount larger than the exposure in that currency. This was taken care of by the fourth set of constraints of the model (see chapter VII, p. 67) which specified that for every currency the total amount of hedging per currency across the three markets had to be less or equal to the original exposure. In fact, this constraint prohibits any form of cross-hedging (also often called "parallel" hedging); i.e., engaging in a forward exchange contract, for example, for a particular currency to hedge the exposure in another currency whose price movements are highly correlated to those of the currency of the hedging transaction. Especially, since hedging costs are

100

very different among currencies and methods of hedging, cross-hedging allows to take advantage of cheaper hedging transactions in some currencies to cover exposures in other currencies of the portfolio exploiting the covariances among them.

In order to allow for cross-hedging, the constraints on the decision variables of the model were relaxed as follows. First, to avoid the eventuality that some decision variables (i.e., amount to be hedged per currency in a particular market) would exceed any tradable volume of foreign currency, new upper bounds were set on the hedging transactions for every currency individually. For this purpose, estimates made by the foreign exchange department of the bank with which Exa does most of its hedging operations were used. These new maxima are volumes for foreign exchange transactions executable in the morning when European foreign exchange markets are open and would, if carefully executed, not move the rate (i.e., hedging cost) of the transactions. These new upper bounds are $ 50 million for all major European currencies plus the C$, $ 20 million for the Yen, $ 10 million for the Skandinavian currencies, A$ and SP and only $ 5 million for the A$.

However, because Exa puts such a strong emphasis on leaving local lines of credit open as a source of short-term financing and the subordination of foreign exchange management to the true business operations of the company, the upper bounds on hedging in the local money market were left at ninety percent of the outstanding lines of credit.

Secondly, the maximum amount of total hedging in any currency should be in function of the size of the original exposure in that currency. Therefore, the righthand side of the constraint on the total amount hedged in any one currency across the three markets (i.e., constraint (5) in the model, see chapter VII, p. 67) will be specified as multiples of the original exposure per currency, i.e., 1.5 times, 2 times and 3 times the original exposure.

The efficient frontiers and variance-hedging costs curves have been derived and are represented in the Figures 19 and 20. The curves are denoted as follows:

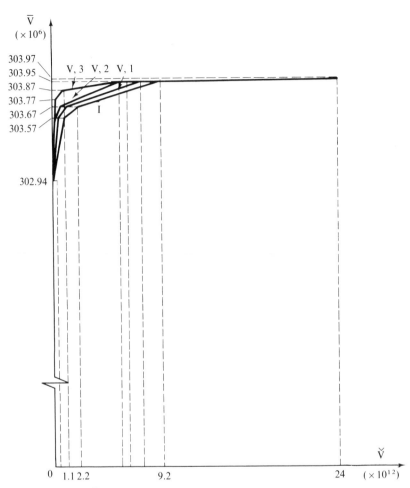

Figure 19. *Efficient Frontier*

Maximum amount hedged per currency	= 1 ×	Original exposure in that currency	: I (original data case)
„	= 1.5 ×	„	: V, 1
„	= 2 ×	„	: V, 2
„	= 3 ×	„	: V, 3

Since it is impossible to list all data on the axes of the curves, a sample of the results is summarised in table 10 below.

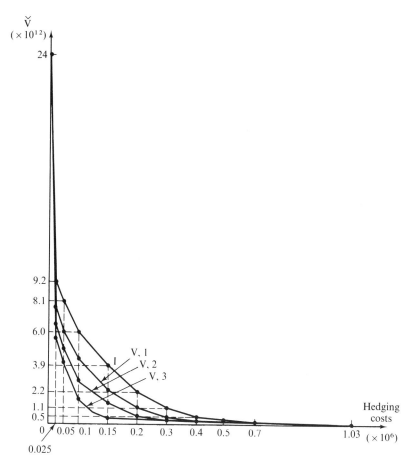

Figure 20. *Variance-hedging Costs Relationships*

An illustrative example of a complete computer run with input and output description is given for the point on Curve V, 1 with total incurred hedging costs equal to $ 200,000. See Appendix V.

The curves representing the relationship between the variance of the foreign exchange portfolio and hedging costs incurred (see Figure 20) shift downward towards the origin of the axes as the upper bounds on the maximum amount of total hedging transactions per currency are increased. This means that it becomes cheaper to reduce the risk of the portfolio as more hedging is done in

103

Table 10. *Portfolio Variance for Different Amounts of Hedging Costs*

Portfolio Variance, $\check{V}$ ($\times 10^{12}$)

Hedging costs	Curve I	Curve V, 1	Curve V, 2	Curve V, 3
0	23.96	23.96	23.96	23.96
25,000	9.22	7.51	6.34	5.78
50,000	8.09	6.11	4.66	4.04
100,000	6.03	4.28	2.92	1.77
150,000	—	—	—	0.96
175,000	—	—	—	0.72
200,000	3.87	2.42	1.44	0.40
300,000	2.22	1.23	0.66	—
400,000	1.08	0.57	0.43	—
500,000	0.50	0.34	0.33	—

some particularly "interesting" currencies. However, cross-hedging does not offer much benefits at both the upper and lower end of the variance. In fact, in the case of Exa, cross-hedging becomes interesting only if one wants to reduce the variance of its foreign exchange portfolio by more than fifty percent. Besides, it is theoretically impossible to fully hedge (i.e., zero variance) at a lower total cost than when no cross-hedging is allowed, the reason being simply that the covariance matrix is by nature positive definite, so that the variance of the portfolio never can become zero, except when hedging transactions are undertaken for every currency in the portfolio for an amount exactly equal to the original exposure. Notice that the variance can be rewritten in matrix notation as follows:

$$\check{V} = [(x_1 - h_1)(x_2 - h_2) \cdots (x_{15} - h_{15})]$$
$$\times \begin{bmatrix} \text{Covariance} \\ \\ \text{matrix} \end{bmatrix} \times \begin{bmatrix} x_1 - h_1 \\ \vdots \\ x_{15} - h_{15} \end{bmatrix}$$

so that $\check{V}$ can only obtain zero value when all currency exposures are fully hedged, i.e., $X_i = h_i$ for all i.[1]

---

1. A theoretical proof by means of a simple two currency example is given in Appendix VI.

Notwithstanding the fact that the zero-variance solution involves an equal amount of total hedging costs (i.e., $ 1,033,660), considerable cost reductions can be obtained in reducing the variance to a very low level by making use of cross-hedging. The following two tables and figures illustrate these savings in hedging costs due to cross-hedging, for some sample points in the relevant range of the portfolio's variance.

Table 11. *Hedging Costs Incurred for Reducing the Variance to a Specified Level (in $)*

Variance $\check{V}$ ($\times 10^{12}$)	I	Hedging costs		
		V, 1	V, 2	V, 3
6.0	100,000	56,000	33,000	20,000
5.0	153,000	83,000	50,000	33,000
4.0	200,000	120,000	80,000	50,000
3.0	250,000	165,000	100,000	73,000
2.0	315,000	225,000	160,000	95,000
1.0	400,000	300,000	235,000	140,000
0.5	500,000	400,000	300,000	190,000

Table 12. *Savings in Hedging Costs Due to Cross-hedging with Respect to the Original Data Case (i.e., no Cross-hedging)*

Variance $\check{V}$ ($\times 10^{12}$)	Savings in Hedging Costs		
	V, 1	V, 2	V, 3
6.0	44,000	67,000	80,000.
5.0	70,000	103,000	120,000
4.0	80,000	120,000	150,000
3.0	85,000	150,000	177,000
2.0	90,000	155,000	220,000
1.0	100,000	165,000	260,000
0.5	100,000	200,000	310,000

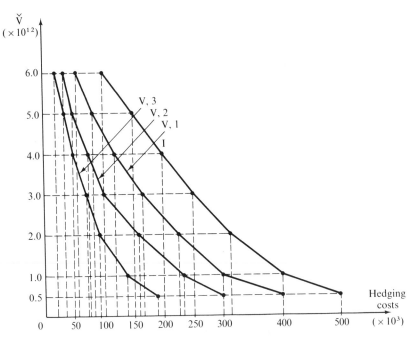

Figure 21. *Variance-hedging Costs Relationships for the* (6.0–0.5)
Segment of Exa's Foreign Exchange Portfolio's Variance

The savings in hedging costs due to cross-hedging are, however, a decreasing function of the upper bound on the total amount of hedging in every currency. Moreover, the new upper bounds on the individual hedging methods might become more binding; and taking large positions (short positions in the case of Exa) in particular currencies might easily be interpreted by the company's managers as a form of foreign exchange speculation.

The composition of the optimal mix of hedging transactions naturally differs as the upper bounds on the maximum amount of hedging in any currency are relaxed. In order to demonstrate this shift in the mix of selected hedging transactions, consider the selection of hedges at $20,000 total hedging costs for the original data and cross-hedging cases with the upper bound on hedging any currency equal to 1.5 times the original exposure.

106

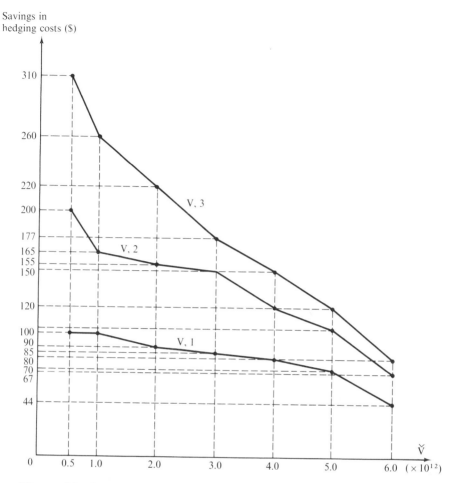

Figure 22. *Savings in Hedging Costs Due to Cross-hedging in Comparison with the Original Data Case (i.e., no Cross-hedging)*

Table 13. *Selected Mix of Hedging Transactions at $200,000 Total Hedging Costs without (Case I) and with Cross-Hedging (Case V, 1)*

Currency	Case I		Case V, 1	
	Forward market	Euro-market	Forward market	Euro-market
A$	8,333		8,380	
BF	121,830		183,000	
C$	82,200		82,200	
DG		36,800		55,146
DK	13,210		20,000	
DM		31,000		27,187
NK	10,570		15,800	
PS	576	37,800		37,796
SF	31,390		47,070	

Although the same nine currencies appear in the selected mix of hedging transactions, in the case of cross-hedging, however, five currencies (i.e., BF, DG, DK, NK, SF) enter at their new upper bound. This means that the model recommends to take on a net short position in these five currencies, as one hedges for a larger amount of the original (long) exposure. But, this leads to a reduction of the variance of the foreign exchange portfolio to 2.44×10^{12}, in contrast to 3.87×10^{12} in the case where no cross-hedging is allowed, with the same total hedging costs ($200,000).

The fact that the upper bound on the amount hedged in the local money market was left unchanged at ninety percent of the outstanding lines of credit, did not curtail the selection of the optimal mix of hedging transactions, as the first (and only) hedge in the local money market enters at total hedging costs equal to $500,000 (the variance is then already down to 0.34×10^{12} from 24×10^{12}). This implies that there is very little benefit to deviate from Exa's policy not to extend local lines of credit for pure reasons of hedging foreign exchange exposure.

Chapter X

Conclusions

The portfolio approach to foreign exchange exposure management makes an explicit consideration of the inherent relationship among the currencies in the company's foreign currency portfolio. Application of the portfolio hedging model resulted in the following findings:

—When hedging costs are measured correctly, i.e., the sum of transaction costs and the difference between the forward rate and one's forecast of the future spot rate, one can substantially reduce the variance of the company's foreign exchange portfolio at very low cost.

—Further substantial reductions in these already small hedging costs can be achieved using cross-hedging, i.e., engaging in a hedging transaction for a particular currency to hedge the exposure in another currency whose price movements are highly correlated to those of the currency of the hedging transaction.

—The principal conclusion is that hedging should be used much more extensively than is the common practice.

These findings are in sharp contrast with the actual practice of most companies' foreign exchange managers. First, most companies interviewed did not explicitly consider their exposure in each foreign currency as part of a portfolio and therefore did not evaluate their position in one currency in terms of their exposure in other currencies. Ignoring the statistical relationship between changes in the exchange rates of the currencies maintained by the company has two major implications: (a) a serious understatement of the true variance of the foreign exchange portfolio or foreign exchange risk to the company; and (b) neglect of the possibility of cross-hedging and of the substantial savings in the hedging costs which can be achieved by cross-hedging. Second, most companies interviewed measured the costs of hedging as the spread between the current spot and forward rates. This procedure results in a substantial over-estimate of the costs of hedging and subsequently an underhedging of the company's foreign exchange risk. Finally, companies do not engage in a sufficient amount of foreign exchange hedging as a result of the misspecification of the costs of hedging.

However, this study solved only part of the foreign exchange problem, i.e., how to protect the dollar value of the foreign currency assets and liabilities against changes in the exchange rates, assuming the exposure in those currencies to be known. This is probably the easy part of the whole foreign exchange problematic. The findings indicate to favor extensive hedging to cover the risks of adverse effects on the company's reported profits and net worth due to changes in the rates of exchange. But the more difficult problem of assessing the end-of-period value of the foreign exchange exposure taking into account the effects of the changes in exchange rates on this value remains unsolved and is suggested as an area for further research.

Appendices

Appendix I

Exchange Rates to be Used for Translating Balance Sheet Accounts Under the FASB No. 8

	Translation Rates	
	Current	Historical
ASSETS		
Cash on hand, demand and time deposits	×	
Marketable equity securities:		
Carried at cost		×
Carried at current market price	×	
Accounts and notes receivables, related unearned discount	×	
Allowance for doubtful accounts and notes receivable	×	
Inventories:		
Carried at cost		×
Carried at current replacement price or current selling price	×	
Carried at net realizable value	×	
Carried at contract price (produced under fixed price contracts)	×	
Prepaid insurance, advertising, and rent		×
Refundable deposits	×	
Advances to unconsolidated subsidiaries	×	
Property, plant, and equipment		×
Accumulated depreciation of property, plant and equipment		×
Cash surrender value of life insurance	×	
Patents, trademarks, licenses, formulas		×
Goodwill		×
Other intangible assets		×
LIABILITIES		
Accounts and notes payable and overdrafts	×	
Accrued expenses payable	×	
Accrued losses on firm purchase commitments	×	
Refundable deposits	×	
Deferred income		×
Bonds payable or other long-term debt	×	

	Translation Rates	
	Current	Historical
LIABILITIES (*cont.*)		
Unamortized premium or discount on bonds or notes payable	×	
Convertible bonds payable	×	
Accrued pension obligations	×	
Obligations under warranties	×	

Source: Financial Accounting Standards Board, *Statement of Financial Accounting Standards* No. 8 [October 1975] Stamford, CT, p. 20.

Appendix II

Assessing Currency Covariances Conditional Upon Economic Variables

Exchange rates, like stock market prices, are aggregates of many factors, including political, administrative and behavioral, as well as economic elements. However, unlike stock market prices, exchange rate changes can be imposed by government action. In fact, an exchange rate is simply the price of a foreign currency in terms of the domestic currency. It reflects the usual market forces of supply and demand, and also central bank intervention. First it is necessary to determine what parameters are relevant to explain the demand and supply for a particular foreign currency. Since Balance of Payments data are designed to show the primary causes of currency supply and demand, studying these Balance of Payments accounts provides clues to future currency prices. The approach looks for factors which the manager in charge of corporate foreign exchange exposure should watch. The final objective is to develop conditional joint probability distributions of currency adjustments across time conditional upon the assessed real factors. The analysis is limited to include only economic variables; this excludes the difficulty of quantifying the political bias towards exchange rate changes. Economic factors for forecasting currency fluctuations have been discussed in business literature (i.e., see Murenbeeld [59], Porter [64], Goeltz [35], Shulman [78]). The objective is to derive conditional joint probability distributions of the changes in exchange rates with respect to real economic variables. Then, a conditional covariance matrix will be derived. Let $\underline{z}$ denote a vector which can be partitioned into two vectors $\underline{z}_1$ and $\underline{z}_2$ representing the monthly changes in exchange rates for the ten currencies and the economic variables respectively.

Then,

$$\underline{\tilde{z}} = \begin{bmatrix} z_1 \\ z_2 \\ z_3 \\ \vdots \\ z_p \\ z_{p+1} \\ \cdot \\ z_n \end{bmatrix} = \begin{bmatrix} \underline{\tilde{z}}_1 \\ \underline{\tilde{z}}_2 \end{bmatrix} \begin{array}{l} \text{changes in exchange rates} \\[1em] \text{economic variables} \end{array}$$

Let f_1 be the marginal mass function of $\underline{\tilde{z}}_1$, so that f_1 in vector notation is equal to $f_{1, 2, 3, \ldots, p}$ in scalar notation; and let $f_{2|1}$ denote the conditional mass function of $\underline{\tilde{z}}_2$ given z_1; then the joint mass function is:

$$f(\underline{z}) = f(\underline{z}_1, \underline{z}_2) = f_1(\underline{z}_1) \times f_{2|1}(\underline{z}_2 | \underline{z}_1)$$

The variance of matrix $\underline{\tilde{z}}$ can be partitioned as followed:

$$V(\underline{\tilde{z}}) = \underline{\check{Z}} = \begin{bmatrix} \underline{\check{z}}_{11} & \underline{\check{z}}_{12} \\ \underline{\check{z}}_{21} & \underline{\check{z}}_{22} \end{bmatrix}$$

where

$$\check{z}_{ii} = E(\tilde{z}_i - \bar{z}_i)^2 \equiv V(\tilde{z}_i)$$

$$\check{z}_{ij} \equiv V(\tilde{z}_i, \tilde{z}_j) \equiv E[(\tilde{z}_i - \bar{z}_i)(\tilde{z}_j - \bar{z}_j)]$$

$$= \text{covariance of } \tilde{z}_i \text{ with } \tilde{z}_j$$

$\underline{\check{Z}}_{11}$ is (px)

then,

$$\underline{\check{Z}}_{ij} = V(\underline{\check{z}}_i, \underline{\check{z}}_j) = E[(\underline{\tilde{z}}_i - \bar{z}_i) \times (\underline{\tilde{z}}_j - \bar{z}_j)]$$

$$= \text{covariance of } \underline{\tilde{z}}_i \text{ and } \underline{\tilde{z}}_j$$

The conditional variance of $\underline{\tilde{z}}_1$ given z_2 is then,

$$V(\underline{\tilde{z}}_1 | z_2) = \underline{\check{z}}_{11} - \underline{\check{z}}_{12} \underline{\check{z}}_{22}^{-1} \underline{\check{z}}_{21}$$

The tests are done for a series of ten currencies, i.e., A\$, BF, C\$, DG, DM, FF, IL, PS, SF and Yen. The data base is retrieved from the International Financial Statistics tapes (furnished by the IMF)

116

for the period February 1973–February 1976. A computer program was written to derive the full covariance matrix; in a next step the AQD-Matpack Program (developed at the Harvard Business School by Professors Glauber and Jones) was used to compute the conditional covariance matrix, $V(\breve{\underline{Z}}_1 | \underline{Z}_2)$.

The conditional covariance matrix has been derived using the following economic variables: relative inflation rates,[1] money supply, and international reserves. All three variables are expressed as a ratio of the current month over the previous month data (e.g., $M_s(t)/M_s(t-1)$, etc.) so as to allow comparability of these values among several countries.

First a (40×40) covariance matrix was derived (i.e., four variables in total for the ten currencies); then this matrix was partitioned into four submatrices:

$\Delta(\text{X.R})$	M_s	Intl. Res.	W.P.I.
10 curr.	10 curr.	10 curr.	10 curr.

z_{11}	z_{12}	
I D E M		
z_{21}	z_{22}	

---

1. Both the consumer price index and the wholesale price index could be used to measure the relative price changes. None of both measures proved to be superior in previous studies. The wholesale price index is used because it was most often used in other similar tests.

where,

z_{11} is a (10×10) matrix
z_{12} is a (10×30) matrix
z_{21} is a (30×10) matrix
z_{22} is a (30×30) matrix
$\Rightarrow V(\tilde{z}_1 | \tilde{z}_2)$ is a (10×10) matrix

Finally, the conditional covariance matrix of absolute changes in the exchange rates of the ten currencies conditional upon the proportional changes in the economic variables, i.e.,

$$V\left(\text{X.R.}(t) - \text{X.R.}(t-1) \middle| \frac{M_s(t)}{M_s(t-1)}, \frac{\text{Intl. Res.}(t)}{\text{Intl. Res.}(t-1)}, \frac{\text{W.P.I.}(t)}{\text{W.P.I.}(t-1)}\right)$$

is derived from $V(\tilde{z}_1 | \tilde{z}_2) = \tilde{z}_{11} - \tilde{z}_{12}\tilde{z}_{22}^{-1}\tilde{z}_{21}$. Applying the same solution procedure the conditional covariance matrix, using relative changes in exchange rates, has also been derived; i.e.,

$$V\left(\frac{\text{X.R.}(t)}{\text{X.R.}(t-1)} \middle| \frac{M_s(t)}{M_s(t-1)}, \frac{\text{Intl. Res.}(t)}{\text{Intl. Res.}(t-1)}, \frac{\text{W.P.I.}(t)}{\text{W.P.I.}(t-1)}\right)$$

The resulting covariance matrices were transformed into correlation matrices (i.e., $\rho_{ij} = \text{cov}_{ij}/\sigma_i\sigma_j$). The latter are represented on page 119.

In order to evaluate these conditional correlations between exchange rate changes, the historical unconditional correlations between the ten currencies were also computed for the same time period. The results for the exchange rate changes specified in absolute and relative terms are given on page 120.

Table II.1. *Correlation matrix of absolute changes in exchange rates, conditional upon M_s, International Reserves, and WPI*

	A$	BF	C$	DG	DM	FF	IL	PS	SF	Y
A$	1.0									
BF	−0.110	1.0								
C$	−0.054	0.772	1.0							
DG	0.079	0.930	0.832	1.0						
DM	0.497	0.673	0.449	0.791	1.0					
FF	−0.239	0.978	0.789	0.858	0.547	1.0				
IL	0.215	0.620	0.714	0.540	0.385	0.659	1.0			
PS	0.008	0.004	0.001	0.003	0.005	0.004	0.006	1.0		
SF	−0.277	0.783	0.532	0.707	0.381	0.739	0.472	0.005	1.0	
Y	−0.148	0.376	0.162	0.335	0.504	0.386	0.266	0.008	0.334	1.0

Table II.2. *Correlation matrix of relative changes in exchange rates, conditional upon M_s, International Reserves, and WPI*

	A$	BF	C$	DG	DM	FF	IL	PS	SF	Y
A$	1.0									
BF	0.116	1.0								
C$	0.070	0.664	1.0							
DG	0.203	0.717	0.976	1.0						
DM	0.183	0.818	0.819	0.812	1.0					
FF	0.503	0.532	0.099	0.265	0.265	1.0				
IL	0.213	−0.055	0.532	0.468	0.139	−0.084	1.0			
PS	0.303	−0.638	−0.318	−0.251	−0.610	−0.291	0.097	1.0		
SF	−0.310	0.526	0.077	0.210	0.066	0.587	−0.372	−0.346	1.0	
Y	−0.315	−0.204	−0.123	−0.127	−0.489	−0.445	−0.032	0.564	0.138	1.0

Table II.3. *Unconditional historical correlation matrix of absolute changes in exchange rates*

	A$	BF	C$	DG	DM	FF	IL	PS	SF	Y
A$	1.0									
BF	0.437	1.0								
C$	0.080	0.234	1.0							
DG	0.476	0.969	0.206	1.0						
DM	0.309	0.707	0.036	0.720	1.0					
FF	0.359	0.880	0.029	0.856	0.639	1.0				
IL	0.181	0.514	−0.260	0.551	0.363	0.609	1.0			
PS	0.291	0.759	0.294	0.731	0.610	0.625	0.432	1.0		
SF	0.431	0.861	0.241	0.851	0.642	0.745	0.430	0.616	1.0	
Y	0.393	0.643	0.192	0.634	0.439	0.670	0.490	0.614	0.641	1.0

Table II.4. *Unconditional historical correlation matrix of relative changes in exchange rates*

	A$	BF	C$	DG	DM	FF	IL	PS	SF	Y
A$	1.0									
BF	0.384	1.0								
C$	0.061	0.224	1.0							
DG	0.398	0.936	0.226	1.0						
DM	0.307	0.844	0.010	0.800	1.0					
FF	0.315	0.881	0.015	0.813	0.749	1.0				
IL	0.170	0.527	−0.239	0.537	0.697	0.621	1.0			
PS	0.247	0.731	0.308	0.655	0.563	0.603	0.422	1.0		
SF	0.377	0.893	0.231	0.835	0.780	0.798	0.489	0.639	1.0	
Y	0.334	0.599	0.178	0.556	0.510	0.633	0.514	0.599	0.604	1.0

The same statistical approach has been applied to assess exchange rate covariances conditional upon economic variables, selected according to the monetary approach to the Balance of Payments. The monetary approach[2] states that surpluses or deficits of the Balance of Payments are not determined by relative prices or interest rates, but by consumers adjusting their desired money balances. Surpluses (deficits) in the money account measure the rate at which monetary balances are being accumulated (reduced) domestically. Since under a system of floating exchange rates no inter-country movements in international reserves occur, the adjustment of actual money balances to their desired level is accomplished by changes in domestic prices and the concommitant changes in the exchange rate. The monetary approach has the advantage to analyse the total of all "items above the line" instead of placing emphasis on individual subaccounts. It can be erroneous to identify movements in the Balance of Payments subaccounts with movements of the domestic aggregate economic activity. For example, a continued deficit in a country's trade balance need not necessarily have any effect on the domestic economic activity if its imports are offset by a surplus in the capital account (e.g., Switzerland).

According to the monetary approach the exchange rate of a currency is determined by the demand and supply for that currency. In addition to the money supply (M_s) economic variables had to be included to reflect money demand. Demand for money is defined to be a function of real income and interest rates. Because no monthly GNP data are available for foreign countries, industrial production (seasonally adjusted) was used as a proxy for GNP. Commercial bank deposit rates (furnished by Morgan Guaranty Trust Company in its monthly *World Financial Markets* publication) are used as short-term interest rates. The wholesale price index is used as a measure of inflation. Since no data on industrial production were available for Belgium and Switzerland, both countries were left out of this analysis.

The conditional covariance matrix for absolute changes in end-of-month exchange rates is thus:

$$V\left(\text{X.R.}(t) - \text{X.R.}(t-1)\,\middle|\, \frac{M_s(t)}{M_s(t-1)}, \frac{\text{Ind. Prod.}(t)}{\text{Ind. Prod.}(t-1)},\right.$$

$$\left.\frac{\text{W.P.I.}(t)}{\text{W.P.I.}(t-1)}, \frac{\text{Int. rate}(t)}{\text{Int.}(t-1)}\right)$$

---

2. For a more detailed analysis of the monetary approach to the BOP see Johnson [42], Kemp [45], and Whitman [87].

The conditional covariance matrix for relative changes in the exchange rates is:

$$V\left(\frac{\text{X.R.}(t)}{\text{X.R.}(t-1)}\middle|\frac{M_s(t)}{M_s(t-1)}, \frac{\text{Ind. Prod.}(t)}{\text{Ind. Prod.}(t-1)},\right.$$

$$\left.\frac{\text{W.P.I.}(t)}{\text{W.P.I.}(t-1)}, \frac{\text{Int. Rates}(t)}{\text{Int. Rates}(t-1)}\right)$$

The resulting correlation matrices are represented in Tables II.5 and II.6.

Table II.5. *Conditional covariance matrix of absolute changes in exchange rates*

	A$	C$	DG	DM	FF	IL	PS	Y
A$	1.0							
C$	−0.798	1.0						
DG	0.240	0.060	1.0					
DM	0.087	−0.146	0.797	1.0				
FF	0.512	−0.189	0.953	0.755	1.0			
IL	0.914	−0.624	0.611	0.388	0.808	1.0		
PS	−0.065	0.451	0.908	0.641	0.788	0.319	1.0	
Y	−0.034	0.015	0.775	0.975	0.711	0.274	0.704	1.0

Table II.6. *Conditional covariance matrix of relative changes in exchange rates*

	A$	C$	DG	DM	FF	IL	PS	Y
A$	1.0							
C$	−0.804	1.0						
DG	−0.189	0.365	1.0					
DM	0.552	−0.318	0.705	1.0				
FF	0.471	−0.169	0.716	0.957	1.0			
IL	0.905	−0.621	0.241	0.847	0.793	1.0		
PS	−0.091	0.435	0.926	0.703	0.805	0.329	1.0	
Y	−0.073	0.018	0.709	0.628	0.721	0.261	0.696	1.0

Although interesting, the results of these tests have little practical usefulness for the money manager because: (a) the conditional correlation matrix is not diagonal. Ideally, the conditional matrix should have been diagonal, which would mean that the correlation between the ten currencies is fully explained by the conditioning economic variables. The relatively large off-diagonal elements reflect the presence of the European snake effect. (b) Even if the off-diagonal elements turned out to be very small, it would be almost impossible to assess the conditioning variables. How would the manager forecast the M_s and M_d components and especially the covariances between them? For example, if short-term interest rates in Germany rise, what will happen to the money supply, wholesale price index, etc. in France, Belgium, . . .? Bypassing this problem (as is done in the tests) using historical data for the conditional variables and assessing exchange rate changes conditional upon them, is only as good (at best) as using the true historical exchange rate fluctuations.

This limited statistical evidence has proven that the analysis of economic variables (Balance of Payments components and/or the fundamental factors affecting the demand for and supply of foreign exchange) has little practical value for forecasting covariances between exchange rates.

Appendix III

Data Resources Used for Exchange Rate Forecasting Based on the Fisher Theorem

The Fisher theorem has been applied to the following set of seventeen foreign currencies: AS, A$, BF, C$, DG, DK, DM, FF, IL, NK, PE, PS, SAR, SF, SK, SP, and Y.

All spot exchange rates were retrieved from the IMF's monthly issue of *International Financial Statistics*. The three month local interest rates on assets denominated in the foreign currencies were sourced as follows:

Australia, Belgium, Denmark, Japan, Norway, South Africa, Sweden: *World Financial Markets* published by Morgan Guaranty Trust Company, New York.

Canada, Germany, The Netherlands, U.K.: *Federal Reserve Bulletin.*

Austria, France, Italy, Portugal, Spain, Switzerland: *Financial Statistics* published by the OECD.

All spot exchange and money market rates are end-of-month quotations, covering the period June 1971–December 1976.

124

Appendix IV

Portfolio Model for the Exa Company

Objective Function

$$\text{Min } \check{V}(\eta_{1,i}, \eta_{2,i}, \eta_{3,i}) = \sum_{i=1}^{15} \sum_{j=1}^{15} \bar{s}_{1,i}$$
$$\times [G_i - \eta_{1,i} - (1 + r_i)\eta_{2,i} - (1 + R_i)\eta_{3,i}]$$
$$\times \bar{s}_{1,j} \times [G_j - \eta_{1,j} - (1 + r_j)\eta_{2,j} - (1 + R_j)\eta_{3,j}]$$
$$\times \text{Cov}(\tilde{s}_{1,i}, \tilde{s}_{1,j})$$

(1)

$$16{,}778{,}523 \leq \eta_{1,1} \leq 92{,}444{,}810$$
$$920{,}471 \leq \eta_{1,2} \leq 11{,}321{,}268$$
$$35{,}971{,}223 \leq \eta_{1,3} \leq 146{,}215{,}000$$
$$1{,}009{,}184 \leq \eta_{1,4} \leq 95{,}074{,}149$$
$$2{,}457{,}002 \leq \eta_{1,5} \leq 49{,}403{,}000$$
$$5{,}787{,}037 \leq \eta_{1,6} \leq 14{,}859{,}000$$
$$2{,}362{,}391 \leq \eta_{1,7} \leq 99{,}772{,}903$$
$$4{,}970{,}179 \leq \eta_{1,8} \leq 93{,}843{,}821$$
$$874{,}890{,}630 \leq \eta_{1,9} \leq 13{,}782{,}700{,}000$$
$$5{,}184{,}033 \leq \eta_{1,10} \leq 11{,}263{,}000$$
$$587{,}406 \leq \eta_{1,11} \leq 45{,}773{,}011$$
$$2{,}450{,}380 \leq \eta_{1,12} \leq 35{,}924{,}200$$
$$4{,}127{,}115 \leq \eta_{1,13} \leq 53{,}067{,}900$$
$$68{,}493{,}150 \leq \eta_{1,14} \leq 219{,}702{,}000$$
$$294{,}117{,}640 \leq \eta_{1,15} \leq 1{,}671{,}090{,}000$$

(2)

$$\eta_{2,1} = 0$$
$$\eta_{2,2} = 0$$

$$\eta_{2,3} = 0$$
$$\eta_{2,4} = 0$$
$$245,700 \le \eta_{2,5} \le 51,614,300$$
$$\eta_{2,6} = 0$$
$$236,239 \le \eta_{2,7} \le 101,899,000$$
$$497,018 \le \eta_{2,8} \le 98,316,982$$
$$\eta_{2,9} = 0$$
$$\eta_{2,10} = 0$$
$$58,741 \le \eta_{2,11} \le 46,301,676$$
$$245,038 \le \eta_{2,12} \le 38,129,500$$
$$\eta_{2,13} = 0$$
$$\eta_{2,14} = 0$$
$$\eta_{2,15} = 0$$

(3)
$$0 \le \eta_{3,1} \le 3,775,168$$
$$0 \le \eta_{3,2} \le 1,242,636$$
$$0 \le \eta_{3,3} \le 8,093,525$$
$$0 \le \eta_{3,4} \le 3,633,061$$
$$0 \le \eta_{3,5} \le 3,538,084$$
$$0 \le \eta_{3,6} \le 156,250$$
$$0 \le \eta_{3,7} \le 14,457,831$$
$$0 \le \eta_{3,8} \le 8,051,690$$
$$0 \le \eta_{3,9} \le 1,732,280,000$$
$$0 \le \eta_{3,10} \le 93,313$$
$$0 \le \eta_{3,11} \le 2,854,793$$
$$0 \le \eta_{3,12} \le 5,072,286$$
$$0 \le \eta_{3,13} \le 2,600,083$$

$$0 \leq \eta_{3,14} \leq \quad 22{,}808{,}219$$

$$0 \leq \eta_{3,15} \leq \quad 423{,}529{,}000$$

(4)
$$0 \leq \eta_{1,1} \; + 1.0725 \quad \times \eta_{3,1} \quad \leq 92{,}444{,}810$$

$$0 \leq \eta_{1,2} \; + 1.0975 \quad \times \eta_{3,2} \quad \leq 11{,}321{,}268$$

$$0 \leq \eta_{1,3} \; + 1.1125 \quad \times \eta_{3,3} \quad \leq 146{,}215{,}000$$

$$0 \leq \eta_{1,4} \; + 1.075 \quad \times \eta_{3,4} \quad \leq 95{,}074{,}149$$

$$0 \leq \eta_{1,5} \; + 1.065 \quad \times \eta_{2,5} \; + 1.08 \times \eta_{3,5} \leq 49{,}141{,}635$$

$$0 \leq \eta_{1,6} \; + 1.135 \quad \times \eta_{3,6} \quad \leq 1{,}485{,}900$$

$$0 \leq \eta_{1,7} \; + 1.055 \quad \times \eta_{2,7} \; + 1.07 \times \eta_{3,7} \leq 99{,}523{,}671$$

$$0 \leq \eta_{1,8} \; + 1.115 \quad \times \eta_{2,8} \; + 1.10 \times \eta_{3,8} \leq 93{,}289{,}646$$

$$0 \leq \eta_{1,9} \; + 1.195 \quad \times \eta_{3,9} \quad \leq 13{,}782{,}700{,}000$$

$$0 \leq \eta_{1,10} + 1.075 \quad \times \eta_{3,10} \leq 11{,}263{,}000$$

$$0 \leq \eta_{1,11} + 1.13875 \quad \times \eta_{2,11} + 1.55 \times \eta_{3,11} \leq 45{,}706{,}340$$

$$0 \leq \eta_{1,12} + 1.044375 \times \eta_{2,12} + 1.0625 \times \eta_{3,12} \leq 35{,}668{,}250$$

$$0 \leq \eta_{1,13} + 1.115 \quad \times \eta_{3,13} \leq 53{,}067{,}900$$

$$0 \leq \eta_{1,14} + 1.095 \quad \times \eta_{3,14} \leq 219{,}702{,}000$$

$$0 \leq \eta_{1,15} + 1.075 \quad \times \eta_{3,15} \leq 1{,}671{,}090{,}000$$

(5)
$$\sum_{i=1}^{15} \left(\bar{s}_{1,i} - {}_0 s_{1,i} + TC_1 \times s_{0,i} \right) \eta_{1,i} + \sum_{i=1}^{15} \left[(1 + r_i) \bar{s}_{1,i} \right.$$

$$- (1 + r_\$) s_{0,i} + TC_2 \times s_{0,i}] \eta_{2,i} + \sum_{i=1}^{15} \left[(1 + R_i) \bar{s}_{1,i} \right.$$

$$- (1 + R_\$) s_{0,i} + TC_3 \times s_{0,i}] \times \eta_{3,i}$$

$$= 304{,}101{,}500 - K = K'.$$

Appendix V

Input/Output Specification Computer Run with $200,000 Total Hedging Costs of Curve V, 1

$$\text{Min } \check{V}(\eta_{1,i}, \eta_{2,i}, \eta_{3,i}) = \sum_{i=1}^{15} \sum_{i=j}^{15} \bar{s}_{1,i}[G_i - \eta_{1,i}$$

$$- (1 + r_i)\eta_{2,i} - (1 + R_i)\eta_{3,i}] \times \bar{s}_{1,j}[G_j - \eta_{1,j}$$

$$- (1 + r_j)\eta_{2,j} - (1 + R_j)\eta_{3,j}] \times \text{cov}(\tilde{s}_{1,i}, \tilde{s}_{1,j})$$

subject to:

(1)	$16{,}778{,}523 \leq \eta_{1,1} \leq$	$167{,}800{,}000$
(2)	$920{,}471 \leq \eta_{1,2} \leq$	$8{,}380{,}000$
(3)	$35{,}971{,}223 \leq \eta_{1,3} \leq$	$1{,}792{,}000{,}000$
(4)	$1{,}009{,}184 \leq \eta_{1,4} \leq$	$82{,}200{,}000$
(5)	$2{,}457{,}002 \leq \eta_{1,5} \leq$	$122{,}700{,}000$
(6)	$5{,}787{,}037 \leq \eta_{1,6} \leq$	$58{,}000{,}000$
(7)	$2{,}362{,}391 \leq \eta_{1,7} \leq$	$121{,}000{,}000$
(8)	$4{,}970{,}179 \leq \eta_{1,8} \leq$	$248{,}500{,}000$
(9)	$874{,}890{,}630 \leq \eta_{1,9} \leq 43{,}554{,}000{,}000$
(10)	$5{,}184{,}033 \leq \eta_{1,10} \leq$	$52{,}000{,}000$
(11)	$587{,}406 \leq \eta_{1,11} \leq$	$43{,}040{,}000$
(12)	$2{,}450{,}380 \leq \eta_{1,12} \leq$	$122{,}500{,}000$
(13)	$4{,}127{,}115 \leq \eta_{1,13} \leq$	$53{,}970{,}000$
(14)	$68{,}493{,}150 \leq \eta_{1,14} \leq$	$685{,}000{,}000$
(15)	$294{,}117{,}640 \leq \eta_{1,15} \leq 5{,}714{,}000{,}000$

$$(16) \qquad \eta_{2,1} = 0$$

$$(17) \qquad \eta_{2,2} = 0$$

128

(18) $\eta_{2,3} = 0$

(19) $\eta_{2,4} = 0$

(20) $245{,}700 \leq \eta_{2,5} \leq 122{,}700{,}000$

(21) $\eta_{2,6} = 0$

(22) $236{,}239 \leq \eta_{2,7} \leq 121{,}800{,}000$

(23) $497{,}018 \leq \eta_{2,8} \leq 248{,}500{,}000$

(24) $\eta_{2,9} = 0$

(25) $\eta_{2,10} = 0$

(26) $58{,}741 \leq \eta_{2,11} \leq 43{,}620{,}000$

(27) $245{,}038 \leq \eta_{2,12} \leq 122{,}500{,}000$

(28) $\eta_{2,13} = 0$

(29) $\eta_{2,14} = 0$

(30) $\eta_{2,15} = 0$

(31) $0 \leq \eta_{3,1} \leq 3{,}780{,}000$

(32) $0 \leq \eta_{3,2} \leq 1{,}240{,}000$

(33) $0 \leq \eta_{3,3} \leq 8{,}090{,}000$

(34) $0 \leq \eta_{3,4} \leq 3{,}630{,}000$

(35) $0 \leq \eta_{3,5} \leq 3{,}530{,}000$

(36) $0 \leq \eta_{3,6} \leq 160{,}000$

(37) $0 \leq \eta_{3,7} \leq 14{,}400{,}000$

(38) $0 \leq \eta_{3,8} \leq 8{,}050{,}000$

(39) $0 \leq \eta_{3,9} \leq 1{,}732{,}000{,}000$

(40) $0 \leq \eta_{3,10} \leq 90{,}000$

(41) $0 \leq \eta_{3,11} \leq 2{,}850{,}000$

(42) $0 \leq \eta_{3,12} \leq 5{,}070{,}000$

(43) $0 \leq \eta_{3,13} \leq 2{,}600{,}000$

(44) $0 \le \eta_{3,14} \le \quad 22{,}800{,}000$

(45) $0 \le \eta_{3,15} \le \quad 423{,}500{,}000$

(46) $0 \le \eta_{1,1} \quad + 1.0725 \quad \times \eta_{3,1} \le 114{,}300{,}000$

(47) $0 \le \eta_{1,2} \quad + 1.0975 \quad \times \eta_{3,2} \le 8{,}380{,}000$

(48) $0 \le \eta_{1,3} \quad + 1.1125 \quad \times \eta_{3,3} \le 183{,}000{,}000$

(49) $0 \le \eta_{1,4} \quad + 1.075 \quad \times \eta_{3,4} \le 82{,}200{,}000$

(50) $0 \le \eta_{1,5} \quad + 1.065 \quad \times \eta_{2,5} \quad + 1.08 \times \eta_{3,5} \le 58{,}800{,}000$

(51) $0 \le \eta_{1,6} \quad + 1.135 \quad \times \eta_{3,6} \le 20{,}000{,}000$

(52) $0 \le \eta_{1,7} \quad + 1.055 \quad \times \eta_{2,7} \quad + 1.07 \times \eta_{3,7} \le 121{,}000{,}000$

(53) $0 \le \eta_{1,8} \quad + 1.115 \quad \times \eta_{2,8} \quad + 1.10 \times \eta_{3,8} \le 128{,}000{,}000$

(54) $0 \le \eta_{1,9} \quad + 1.195 \quad \times \eta_{3,9} \le 17{,}901{,}000{,}000$

(55) $0 \le \eta_{1,10} + 1.075 \quad \times \eta_{3,10} \le 15{,}800{,}000$

(56) $0 \le \eta_{1,11} + 1.13875 \quad \times \eta_{2,11} + 1.55 \times \eta_{3,11} \le 43{,}040{,}000$

(57) $0 \le \eta_{1,12} + 1.044375 \times \eta_{2,12} + 1.0625 \times \eta_{3,12} \\ \le 47{,}070{,}000$

(58) $0 \le \eta_{1,13} + 1.115 \quad \times \eta_{3,13} \le 53{,}970{,}000$

(59) $0 \le \eta_{1,14} + 1.095 \quad \times \eta_{3,14} \le 286{,}000{,}000$

(60) $0 \le \eta_{1,15} + 1.075 \quad \times \eta_{3,15} \le 2{,}327{,}000{,}000$

(61) $$\sum_{i=1}^{15} (\bar{s}_{1,i} - {}_0 s_{1,i} + TC_1 \times s_{0,i})\eta_{1,i} + \sum_{i=1}^{15} [(1 + r_i)\bar{s}_{1,i}$$

$$- (1 + r_\$)s_{0,i} + TC_2 \times s_{0,i}]\eta_{2,i} + \sum_{i=1}^{15} [(1 + R_i)\bar{s}_{1,i}$$

$$- (1 + R_\$)s_{0,i} + TC_3 \times s_{0,i}] \times \eta_{3,i} = \$200{,}000.$$

Output

The decision variables are numbered in sequence per method of hedging, i.e., $\eta_{1,i}$'s correspond to variables numbered 1 to 15, $\eta_{2,i}$'s to 16 through 30, $\eta_{3,i}$'s to 31 through 45.

130

Variable	Value	Upper Bound	Dual	(all values × 10³)

BASIC:

—Not at Upper Bound:

Variable	Value	Upper Bound	Dual
3	183000	1792000	0
4	82200	82200	0
6	20000	58000	0
10	15800	52000	0
12	47070	122500	0
20	55146.5	122700	0
22	27187.1	121800	0
26	37795.8	43620	0

—At Upper Bound:

Variable	Value	Upper Bound	Dual
2	@	8380	-0.501683
16	@	0	-5.70752
17	@	0	-104.037
18	@	0	-2.67181
19	@	0	-95.0837
21	@	0	-16.5479
24	@	0	-0.100809
25	@	0	-18.4728
28	@	0	-23.5866
29	@	0	-1.39815
30	@	0	-0.335173

Constraint	Slack/Surplus	Dual
1	114300	0
2	$2.19424E-5$	0
3	$+0$	$-1.19655E-2$
4	$+0$	$-5.37406E-2$
5	$+0$	-0.198264
6	$+0$	$-2.85462E-2$
7	92317.6	0
8	128000	0

131

9	17901000	0
10	+0	$-3.03389E-2$
11	+0	-0.48551
12	+0	-0.194577
13	53970	0
14	286000	0
15	2327000	0
	$-0-$	-91.6443

Note: The optimal value of a dual variable (often called shadow price) indicates how much the objective function, the variance of the foreign exchange portfolio, changes with a unit change in the associated righthand-side constant. For example, the value of dual variable number 2 is -502, which means that if the righthand-side constant of the constraint on variable 2 is increased by one unit (i.e., to 8,381,000) the variance of the foreign currency portfolio will decrease by 502.

Appendix VI

Proof that Cross-hedging Cannot Reduce Variance To Zero At Lower Costs

The following two currency example is meant to prove that although cross-hedging costs can lead to substantial savings in hedging costs in reducing the variance of the foreign exchange portfolio, it does not allow to attain zero variance at lower costs than without cross-hedging.

Consider two currencies x and y, with original net exposures X and Y.

The covariance matrix of x and y is:

$$\begin{bmatrix} a & b \\ b & c \end{bmatrix}$$

where

$$a = \rho_{x,x} \times \sigma_x \times \sigma_x = 1 \times \sigma_x^2$$
$$c = \rho_{y,y} \times \sigma_y \times \sigma_y = 1 \times \sigma_y^2$$
$$b = \rho_{x,y} \times \sigma_x \times \sigma_y$$

The variance of the portfolio is then:

$$[X \quad Y]\begin{bmatrix} a & b \\ b & c \end{bmatrix}\begin{bmatrix} X \\ Y \end{bmatrix}$$
$$= aX^2 + 2bYX + cY^2$$

Assume that for any given value of Y, we want to find the value of X which reduces the variance of the portfolio to zero. Therefore, we solve the quadratic equation:

$$aX^2 + 2bYX + cY^2 = 0$$
$$X = \frac{-2b \pm Y\sqrt{4b^2 - 4ac}}{2a}$$

This has a solution if $b^2 \geq ac$ or $b \geq \sqrt{a} \times \sqrt{c}$, but

$$b = \rho_{x,y} \times \sigma_x \times \sigma_y = \rho_{x,y} \times \sqrt{a} \times \sqrt{d}$$

Since the covariance matrix is positive definite, there are no real value solutions to the quadratic equation. Hence, there is no combination of X and Y to reduce the variance to zero, except $X = Y = 0$.

There is nothing special about the two-currency case, the n-currency case can easily be derived by mathematical deduction.

Bibliography

[1]   Aliber, R., The Firm under Fixed and Flexible Exchange Rates, paper presented at Seminar on Flexible Exchange Rates and Stabilization Policy, Stockholm, Sweden, 26 August 1975.

[2]   Aliber, R., "The Interest Parity Theorem: A Reinterpretation," *Journal of Political Economy*, November–December 1973, pp. 1451–1459.

[3]   Aliber, R., "Monetary Independence Under Floating Exchange Rates," *Journal of Finance*, Vol. 30, No. 2, May 1975, pp. 365–376.

[4]   Aliber, R., and Stickney, C., "Accounting Measures of Foreign Exposure: The Long and the Short of it," *The Accounting Review*, January 1975, pp. 44–57.

[5]   Ankrom, R., "Top-level Approach to the Foreign Exchange Problem," *Harvard Business Review*, July–August 1974, pp. 79–90.

[6]   Auten, J., "Forward Exchange Rates and Interest Rate Differentials," *The Journal of Finance*, March 1963, pp. 11–19.

[7]   Baglini, N., Risk Management in International Corporations, Risk Studies Foundation, Inc., New York, 1976.

[8]   Balassa, B., "The Purchasing-Power Parity Doctrine: A Reappraisal," *The Journal of Political Economy*, December 1964, pp. 584–96.

[9]   Bilson, J., Rational Expectations and the Exchange Rates: Theory and Estimation, manuscript, Northwestern University, 1975.

[10] Blank, G., "Currency Devaluation: A Guide to Income Tax Consequences in 14 Countries," *Journal of Taxation*, July 1971, pp. 15–19.

[11] Business International Corporation, Hedging Foreign Exchange Risks, New York, No. 49, 1971.

[12] Calman, R., *Linear Programming and Cash Management—Cash Alpha*, The M.I.T. Press, Cambridge, MA, 1968.

[13] Chown, J., *Taxation and Multinational Enterprise*, Longman, London, 1974.

[14] Chown, Kelen and Marcheal, "Hedging Balance Sheet Exposure After Tax—A Reply," *Euromoney*, June 1975.

[15] Curtiss, D., "Hedging Balance-Sheet Exposure After Tax," *Euromoney*, April 1975, pp. 76–77.

[16] Dufey, G., "Corporate Finance and Exchange Rate Variations," *Financial Management*, Summer 1972, pp. 51–57.

[17] Duncan, E., "Lowering the Value of the Dollar Raises Certain Tax Problems," *The Journal of Taxation*, August 1972, pp. 115–119.

[18] Einzig, P., *A Dynamic Theory of Forward Exchange*, 2nd ed., St. Martin Press, New York, 1967.

[19] Ethier, W., "International Trade and the Forward Exchange Market," *The American Economic Review*, June 1973, Vol. 63, No. 3.

[20] Fieleke, N., "Exchange-rate Flexibility and the Efficiency of the Foreign-Exchange Markets," *Journal of Financial and Quantitative Analysis*, September 1975.

[21] Fieleke, W., The 1971 Floatation of the Mark and the Hedging of Commercial Transactions Between the United States and Germany: Experiences of Selected U.S. Non-banking Enterprises.

[22] Financial Accounting Standards Board, Statement of Financial Accounting for the Translation of Foreign Currency Transactions and Foreign Currency Financial Statements, October 1975, Stamford, CT.

[23] Folks, W., "The Optimal Level of Exchange Transactions," *Journal of Financial and Quantitative Analysis*, January 1973, pp. 105–110.

[24] Folks, W. and Stansell, S., "The Use of Discriminant Analysis in Forecasting Exchange Rate Movements," *Journal of International Business Studies*, Spring 1975, pp. 33–50.

[25] Frenkel, J., "Elasticities and the Interest Parity Theory," *Journal of Political Theory*, May–June 1973, pp. 741–747.

[26] Frenkel, J., "A Monetary Approach to the Exchange Rate: Doctrinal Aspects and Empirical Evidence," *Scandinavian Journal of Economics*, 1976.

[27] Frenkel, J. and Levich, R., "Covered Interest Arbitrage: Unexploited Profits?" *Journal of Political Economy*, No. 83, April 1975, pp. 325–338.

[28] Frenkel, J. and Levich, R., "Transaction Costs and Interest Arbitrage: Tranquil Versus Turbulent Periods," *Journal of Political Economy*, Vol. 85, 1977, pp. 1209–1226.

[29] Frommel, S., Taxation of Branches and Subsidiaries in Western Europe, Canada and the U.S.A., Kluwer-Harrap, London, 1975.

[30] Furlong, W., "Minimizing Foreign Exchange Losses," *The Accounting Review*, April 1966, pp. 244–252.

[31] Gaillot, H., "Purchasing Power Parity as an Explanation of Long-term in Exchange Rates," *Journal of Money, Credit and Banking*, Vol. 2, August 1970, pp. 348–357.

[32] Giddy, I. H., "An Integrated Theory of Exchange Rate Equilibrium," *Journal of Financial and Quantitate Analysis*, Vol. XI, No. 5, December 1976, pp. 883–892.

[33] Giddy, I. and Dufey, G., "The Random Behavior of Flexible Exchange Rates: Implications for Forecasting," *Journal of International Business Studies*, Vol. 6, Spring 1975.

[34] Glauber, R., "Modern Investment Theory: Its Implication for Competition Among Financial Institutions," *New England Economic Review*, May–June 1976, pp. 3–13.

[35] Goeltz, R., "Managing Liquid Funds on an International Scale," *Columbia Journal of World Business*, July–August 1972, pp. 59–65.

[36] Grubel, H., "Internationally Diversified Portfolios," *American Economic Review*, December 1968.

[37] Gull, D., "Composite Foreign Exchange Risk," *Columbia Journal of World Business*, Fall 1975, pp. 51–69.

[38] Heckerman, D., "The Exchange Risks of Foreign Operations," *The Journal of Business*, The University of Chicago Press, January 1972, pp. 46–47.

[39] Hekman, C., "Make a Killing in the Foreign Exchange Market—Or Get Killed," *Journal of World Ttade Law*, 1975.

[40] Hoefs, R., "U.S. Taxation of Foreign Income of Americans," *Taxes—The Tax Magazine*, University of Chicago Law School, December 1967.

[41] Holmes, J. M., "The Purchasing Power Parity Theory: In Defense of Gustav Cassel as a Modern Theorist," *Journal of Political Economy*, Vol. 75, October 1967, pp. 686–695.

[42] Johnson, H., *The Monetary Approach to Balance-of-Payments Theory*, in Further Essays in Monetary Economics, Harvard University Press, Cambridge, MA, 1973, pp. 229–249.

[43] Karplus, R., The Monetary Approach to Foreign Exchange Rates: The Current Experience, Term Paper, Graduate School of Business, University of Chicago, November 1975.

[44] Kaserman, D., "The Forward Exchange Rate: Its Determination and Behavior as a Predictor of the Future Spot Rate," *Proceedings of the American Statistical Association*, 1973, pp. 417–422.

[45] Kemp, D., "A Monetary View of the Balance of Payments," *Federal Reserve Bank of St. Louis*, April 1975, pp. 14–22.

[46] Kindleberger, C., *International Economics*, Richard D. Irwin, Inc., Homewood, IL, 1968, p. 40.

[47] Kohlhagen, S., The Foreign Exchange Markets-Model, Tests and Empirical Evidence, Paper presented at U.S. Treasury Conference in Washington, D.C., February 1976.

[48] Kohlhagen, S., The Forward Rate as an Unbiased Predictor of the Future Spot Rate, Mimeograph, University of California, Berkeley, Berkeley, CA, 1974.

[49] Kohlhagen, S., "The Performance of the Foreign Exchange Markets: 1971–1974," *Journal of International Business Studies*, Fall 1975, pp. 33–39.

[50] Levich, R. M., Tests of Forecasting Models and Market Efficiency in the International Money Market, Working Paper No. 75–88, The University of Chicago, August 1976.

[51] Lieberman, G., "Two Ways to Measure Foreign Exchange Risk," *Euromoney*, June 1976, pp. 30–36.

[52] Lietaer, E., *Financial Management of Foreign Exchange*, The M.I.T. Press, Cambridge, MA., 1971.

[53] Lintner, J., "The Valuation of Risk Assets and the Selection of Risky Invest-

ment in Stock Portfolios and Capital Budgets," *Review of Economics and Statistics*, Vol. 47, February 1965, pp. 13–37.

[54] Magee, S., "The Empirical Evidence on the Monetary Approach To the Balance of Payments and Exchange Rates," *American Economic Association*, May 1976, pp. 163–170.

[55] Mandelbrot, B., "Forecasts of Future Prices, Unbiased Markets and Martingale Models," *Journal of Business*, Security Prices: A Supplement, Vol. 39, No. 1, Part 2, January 1966.

[56] Mandlich, D. R., Foreign Exchange Trading Techniques and Controls, American Bankers Association, Washington, D.C., 1976.

[57] Markowitz, H., *Portfolio Selection: Efficient Diversification of Investments*, John Wiley & Sons, Inc., New York, 1959.

[58] Marston, R., "Interest Arbitrage in the Euro-currency Markets," *European Economic Review*, Vol. 7, 1976, pp. 1–13.

[59] Murenbeeld, M., "Economic Factors for Forecasting Foreign Exchange Rate Changes," *Columbia Journal of World Business*, Summer 1975, pp. 81–95.

[60] Officer, L., "The Purchasing-Power-Parity Theory of Exchange Rates: A Review Article," *I.M.F. Staff Papers*, Vol. XXIII, March 1976, pp. 1–60.

[61] Officer, L. and Willett, T., "The Covered Arbitrage Schedule: A Critical Survey of Recent Developments," *Journal of Money, Credit and Banking*, March 1970, pp. 247–257.

[62] Peterson, S., "Impact of Accounting Methods on Foreign Exchange Management," *Euromoney*, June 1974, pp. 50–54.

[63] Pippenger, J., "Spot Rates, Forward Rates and Interest Rate Differentials," *Journal of Money, Credit and Banking*, May 1972, pp. 375–383.

[64] Porter, R., "Forecasting Exchange Rates," *Euromoney*, September 1973, pp. 31–38.

[65] Prachowny, M., "A Note on Interest Parity and the Supply of Arbitrage Funds," *Journal of Political Economy*, Vol. 78, No. 3, May–June 1970.

[66] Price Waterhouse & Company, Corporate Taxes in 80 Countries, July 1976, NY.

[67] Prindl, A., *Foreign Exchange Risk*, John Wiley & Sons, Inc., London, 1976.

[68] Ravenscroft, D., "Taxation of Income Arising from Changes in Value of Foreign Currency," *Harvard Law Review*, Vol. 82, No. 4, February 1969, pp. 772–797.

[69] Ravenscroft, D., "Translating Foreign Currency Under U.S. Tax Laws—An Examination of Five Methods for Translating Foreign Currency into Dollars," *Financial Executive*, September 1974, pp. 58–69.

[70] Ring, T., "The Impact of Taxation on Foreign Exposure," *Euromoney*, January 1976, pp. 82–84.

[71] Robbins, S. and Stobaugh, R., *Money in the Multinational Enterprise*, Longman, London, 1974.

[72] Rodriguez, R. M., "FASB No. 8: What Has It Done For Us?" *Financial Analyst Journal*, March–April 1977, pp. 40–47.

[73] Samuelson, P., "Proof that Properly Anticipated Price Fluctuate Randomly," *Industrial Management Review*, No. 6, 1965, pp. 41–49.
[74] Shapiro, A. C., "Defining Exchange Risk," *Journal of Business*, Vol. 50, No. 1, January 1977, pp. 37–39.
[75] Shapiro, A. C. and Rutenberg, D. P., "Managing Exchange Risks in a Floating World," *Financial Management*, Vol. V, No. 2, pp. 48–57.
[76] Sharpe, W., "Capital Asset Prices: A Theory of Market Equilibrium Under Conditions of Risk," *Journal of Finance*, Vol. 19, September 1964, pp. 425–442.
[77] Sharpe, W., *Portfolio Theory and Capital Markets*, McGraw-Hill Book Co., NY, 1970, p. 48.
[78] Shulman, R., "Are Foreign Exchange Risks Measurable," *Columbia Journal of World Business*, May–June 1970, p. 551.
[79] Sohmen, E., *Flexible Exchange Rates*, University of Chicago Press, 1969.
[80] Solnik, B., *European Capital Markets*, Lexington Books, 1973.
[81] Solnik, B., "Why Not Diversify Internationally Rather Than Domestically?" *Financial Analyst Journal*, July–August 1974, pp. 48–52.
[82] Stein, J., "The Forward Rate and the Interest Parity," *Review of Economic Studies*, April 1965, pp. 113–126.
[83] Teck, A., "Control Your Exposure to Foreign Exchange," *Harvard Business Review*, January–February 1974.
[84] Tsiang, S., "The Theory of Forward Exchange and Effects of Government Intervention on the Forward Exchange Market," *I.M.F. Staff Papers*, Vol. VII, April 1959, pp. 75–106.
[85] Van Agtmael, A., "How Business Has Dealt With Political Risk," *Financial Executive*, January 1976, pp. 26–30.
[86] White, W., "Interest Rate Differences, Forward Exchange Mechanism, and Scope for Short-term Capital Movements," *I.M.F. Staff Papers*, November 1963.
[87] Whitman, M., "Global Monetarism and the Monetary Approach to the Balance of Payments," *Brookings Papers on Economic Activity*, No. 3, 1975, pp. 491–536.

Index

typeset: Santype International Ltd.,
  Salisbury, Wilts
printer: Samsom Sijthoff Grafische
  Bedrijven, Alphen aan den Rijn
binder: Callenbach, Nijkerk
cover-design: W. Bottenheft